Hundred Acre Welcome

Hundred Acre Welcome

THE STORY OF
A CHINCOTEAGUE PONY

RONALD ROOD

Drawings by Robert MacLean

THE STEPHEN GREENE PRESS

BRATTLEBORO, VERMONT · 1967

Printed in the United States of America

Library of Congress catalog card number: 67-18738

To my father and mother, who encouraged my interest in the outdoors as a child, and to my faithful readers who have helped keep this interest alive ever since, this book is gratefully dedicated.

Prove all things; hold fast that which is good.

—I THESSALONIANS V:21

CONTENTS

Books by Ronald Rood

Land Alive

The Loon in My Bathtub

FOR CHILDREN:

Insects We Know

How and Why Wonder Book of Insects

How and Why Wonder Book of Ants and Bees

How and Why Wonder Book of Butterflies and Moths

The Sea and Its Wonderful Creatures

Bees, Bugs and Beetles

CHAPTER ONE

Stargazers

PROBABLY we shouldn't have stopped at that campground. We would have been spared plenty of trouble and not a little money. But we'd have missed a valuable lesson—and a whale of a lot of fun.

The campground itself wasn't any problem. It was what came afterward that got us.

All six of us are fond of traveling, and camping seems to be one of the best ways to see the country. It helps us do the most on my income as a freelance writer and Peg's as a kindergarten teacher. Since my primary writing interest is natural history, I usually hope to parlay each trip into a story for a book or magazine. This may not work forever, but we'll have had a good time trying. In the process we'll have seen a lot of plants and animals and unspoiled country.

Even so, it was going to be good to get home again. We had left Vermont nearly two months earlier on a round trip to the West Coast. I had been getting material for a book on insects, and the rest of my family had been serving as my work crew. They'd discovered locusts and beetles, steadied plants in the wind while I photographed caterpillars clinging to the stems or leaves, and looked up bugs in my field guides.

The particular spot that started the chain of events happened to be on the shore of a lake in Minnesota. The campground directory showed it to be right on our way home, for a three-day swing from there through Sault Ste. Marie and down past Montreal should get us back to our own hundred acres of Vermont woods and meadows.

After we'd parked the car, Peg dug around in our supplies for the supper things. Janice went after some fresh water while Tom picked up the campsite. I tried to coax enough enthusiasm out of our ancient gasoline stove for a batch of pancakes.

Roger and Alison were supposed to clean and set the picnic table. But our two youngest are as human as the rest of us: somebody had left a newspaper on the table, and they busied themselves as much with its contents as with the damp cloth and dishes.

As it turned out, it was an unusual newspaper. They didn't throw it away when they were through, but laid it at one end of the table. When we'd finished our meal, Roger pulled it toward him.

"What'll we do after dishes, Dad?"

I considered my nine-year-old son's question. As far as possible, we like to create our own entertainment instead of having it dished up to us ready-made. Often we explore our new surroundings. We poke along the shore, if there's a lake, or wander through the campground and meet other campers.

Tonight, however, was to be special. I reminded Roger of what we'd discovered in Tom's astronomy book—that if visibility was right we'd see an unusual number of shooting stars.

"But that's not until about midnight, Dad. Couldn't we go to the movie first?"

"What movie, Roger?"

At this point Alison spoke up. "The drive-in theater it tells about in the newspaper. See?"

They opened the paper to a page that listed all the area's theaters and their offerings. Roger pointed to a large ad in the bottom corner.

"You know how we're counting every penny on this trip," I reminded him. "Why's this movie so important?"

"*Misty of Chincoteague?* It's about wild horses."

At this I glanced at my wife. We'd long since found that it usually paid to have a united front. Now, though, I had my doubts. Peg had been brought up practically on horseback, and I might have to go it alone.

"Look, kids," I began, "you've seen lots of movies about horses. And these Perseids only show up once a year. The rest of the time they're millions of miles out in space."

Now Tom joined in. "But the book says they're out for three nights. Can't we watch them tomorrow night? Or maybe Janice could drive us kids to the movies. Then you could stay here and watch shooting stars all you wanted to."

His big sister wasn't quite so confident of her ability as he was. Perhaps they didn't allow sixteen-year-olds to drive at night in Minnesota. Then she brightened. "Look! Why don't we all go to the movies and then watch the Perseids when we get back?"

I considered this for a moment. It might be nice to take in a movie for a change. We'd stuck pretty close to our budget all the way to California and back. As the children pointed out, the price of admission would be only for the car, rather than for each person separately. Besides, the Perseids were better after midnight, anyway.

Peg nodded her approval, and so it was decided. We'd go to the movies. Then, since it promised to be a pleasant night, we could just roll our sleeping bags out on the ground when we got back and look for shooting stars.

The drive-in theater was about three miles away. As we approached it, I could see the huge screen poking up out of the Minnesota countryside. Then, as we got closer, the children suddenly sobered down. There was just one word on the marquee. It looked almost like the word *Closed*; perhaps the projection booth had caught fire or something, and the show couldn't go on.

But no. Now we could see it well. The title of the picture had been shortened to one word. It stood there, innocently enough, in black letters on a white background:

Misty.

The kids were quick to give us all the details of what we'd be seeing. I remembered vaguely about Misty, the forlorn little filly who'd been rescued from the waves on the island of Chincoteague, Virginia. She was the pony-heroine of a story by Marguerite Henry which had been made into a movie. Although I hadn't read the story, the children were familiar with it, and had been hoping to see the film ever since it had been released.

We all enjoyed it. The children, of course, were captivated by the thundering hoofs and the story of the little pony. Peg remarked how nice it must be to swim in those sparkling ocean waters, while I was intrigued by the wild scenery with its waving beach grass and its endless sand dunes. According to my admittedly biased opinion, there could have been a lot more of that scenery. Just as one of the principal characters would get close to the crest of a dune or a scraggly clump of bushes, the picture would change—and there I'd be, wondering what was over the other side of that dune or hidden in those bushes.

The children talked about the movie all the way back to camp. They were still talking after we'd spread out the last sleeping bag on the grass and snapped out the last flashlight.

Now a new show began. Janice and Roger saw the first shooting star—a flicker high overhead. Some particle, plunging into the earth's atmosphere, had burned itself out.

We all saw the next one. We were still looking where Janice had pointed when a great streak sped toward the west, trailing a dotted path of sparks. Its glowing wake hung in the heavens for perhaps three seconds. The annual display of the Perseids was on.

This cluster of interplanetary débris, hurtling on an orbit through space like a swarm of bees, has been thought to be the remains of a comet that exploded before the dawn of man's knowledge. Once a year, about August tenth, eleventh and twelfth, the mass of particles comes within the pull of our gravity. Then a few million bits of its substance rush toward the earth.

Actually, we hadn't missed much of the show, because light and atmospheric conditions are most favorable around midnight. Tom, the family's champion stargazer, counted fifty meteors in the first hour as we lay awake; the rest of us got about forty. They were all over the sky. Some of them came from the constellation Perseus, high in the eastern heavens, from which they get their name, yet no matter where we looked we would soon see a space-traveler meet its fiery death.

During a lull in the silent fireworks, I allowed my eyes to close. But in an instant I was wide awake. Something had tickled me. From below.

I wondered if I'd been imagining things. It was as if a stout finger had jabbed right into my spine as I lay flat on my back. Then, just as I'd decided it had been a dream, the finger jabbed again.

Rolling away in my sleeping bag, I shone the flashlight on the offending spot in the earth. There was nothing but a small hole in the ground, perhaps three inches in diameter. But it recalled for me a little visitor we'd had during supper. Sitting up so straight that it embodied its nickname of Tent Peg, a thirteen-lined ground squirrel had surveyed us as we ate. It reminded us of a chipmunk with dots and dashes instead of a stripe. After dark, when I'd spread my sleeping bag out in the gloom, I had accidentally covered one of its doorways. Even though the little creature usually sleeps at night, my slumbering presence had prompted him to give an experimental poke with his nose.

I shifted my position so as not to coincide so closely with his bedroom, and was settling down once more when a crackling sound made me glance toward the lump of Roger's sleeping bag. From the looks, I figured he must be hidden beneath the covers with his flashlight on. Probably reading, I decided, even if it must be nearly two in the morning.

I called to him quietly.

The noise like rustling paper stopped. I relaxed once more. Then, just as I was dropping off a second time, I heard it again.

"Listen, Roger," I said, "enough's enough. It's nearly two o'clock in the morning. Put away whatever you're reading and don't turn that flashlight on again. Okay?"

Silence. Until, unaccountably, I heard the paper sound a third time.

That did it. I rolled out of bed and went over to that disobedient little lump in the sleeping bag. Taking aim at the most likely part, I let fly with a good swat—and promptly lost my balance. The bag was empty.

I recovered myself, and felt over to Alison's bag. Hers was empty, too. Snatching up the flashlight, I shone it around the campground. There wasn't anybody home but me.

Almost immediately I heard a door open and close. Looking over at our square little bus-type station wagon, I saw its interior lights turned on. My children were in pajamas, poring over a big road map. Peg had just joined them.

"Did they wake you, too?" Peg asked as I entered the station wagon.

"Good heavens, yes," I told her. "First I get routed out of bed by a ground squirrel. Then you fool with that map so it sounds like somebody's reading a newspaper right in my ear. What the deuce are you doing out here, anyway, in the middle of the night?"

For answer, Roger pulled the map over to me. "Daddy, where's Chincoteague? We can't seem to find it."

"Chincoteague? At two o'clock in the morning?"

Nevertheless I dutifully looked with them at Virginia's east coast. Soon, though, we decided that this map showed only the larger towns.

Then I asked what seemed to me to be a logical question. What was so important about its location, anyway, that we had to crowd together in a station wagon under an electric bulb at two in the morning to find it?

For answer, Janice opened the map to its full extent. She showed me our present location. From Minnesota, where we were, it would be a simple thing to swing down to Virginia on our way home, instead of up into Canada as we'd planned. The children, after whispering about this, had decided to clinch their point by going to the car and checking the map. Peg, curious, had followed, and I'd brought up the rear.

There wasn't much we could do now without a proper guide to Virginia, however. So, after promising we'd pick up a good map in the morning when we stopped for gasoline, I managed to get everybody back in sleeping bags.

At last all flashlights were out again. As I blinked at a passing Perseid and listened to the steady throb of the insects, I realized there'd been another good reason for not going to the movies that night: the whole business had ruined a night's sleep.

I realized something else, too. I would have to keep my promise
to get that map. Even in the dark, I could sense that Roger was
lying wide awake in his sleeping bag. But he wasn't just watching
shooting stars. My guess was that he was still watching that movie.

The next morning we discussed our eventful evening as we
yawned our way around the campground. Following a dip in the
lake, we had a quick breakfast, packed the stuff into the station
wagon, and headed east. Our immediate goal was a large cross-
roads service station likely to have maps of distant parts of the
country.

When we found one, though, Chincoteague turned out to be
farther south than we'd figured. It was located well down the Del-
Mar-Va peninsula, which forms the east coast of Chesapeake Bay.
To visit it now would take several extra days, and our budget
would never stand it.

Roger folded the map and solemnly handed it back to the
service station attendant. "We don't need it yet," he announced.
"We're going to Vermont first."

The man watched as we started the engine. Then he walked
around to my side of the car. "Here," he said with a grin as he
handed me the map. "Just in case you change your mind again."

After we got started, things quieted down. Janice snoozed in
the back corner. Tom was busy with a paperback book he'd bought
at the gasoline station. Peg dozed over her notebook, and Roger
and Alison busied themselves with the new map. Getting out our
other maps, they measured time and mileage from Vermont to
Virginia.

If we took the trip, they finally decided, we could leave Vermont early in the morning and make it late that same day. Very
late, they admitted, but we could do it.

So much for the time and distance. No problem at all. Now for
the gasoline.

"How many miles do we get on a gallon?" Alison asked.

"Oh, let's say about twenty on a trip," I answered.

She did some pencil work for a few minutes. "Golly, Dad, you mean it only costs twenty dollars to go twelve hundred miles?"

I told her this was only the first expense, and that gasoline was about the cheapest thing you could put into a car. This was a phrase I got from a used-car salesman. Then, speaking in my best income-tax voice, I explained about the other costs: tires, oil, grease, depreciation—making them sound as grim as I could. Alison dutifully wrote them down.

She was quiet again. Glancing in the rear-view mirror, I could see her doing arithmetic. She'd be daunted, I figured, when she added up all the costs of driving a car; bet she never looked at it in that light before.

She kept at it until Janice stirred a little. Alison poked her fully awake and gave her the figures. I saw my older daughter's brows knit in concentration as she went over Alison's paper. At last they had the answer. The way it came out we could go to Chincoteague for about fifty dollars a week. And the longer we stayed the cheaper it got.

Then Alison played her master card. "In fact, if we stayed there all summer, it'd cost us just a dollar a day. For the whole family."

It was my turn to concentrate. There must be some catch to it somewhere, although the way she'd reasoned it out, it made a certain amount of sense.

In the first place, we had to eat no matter where we were; so we didn't even have to count the cost of food. Next, since we'd be "on location" all summer, we would be using scarcely any gasoline. By the time the summer was over, we might even have used less gas on the Vermont-to-Chincoteague junket than we'd have frittered away in little trips around home.

"We really don't have to figure the cost of gasoline, either,"

Alison concluded. "The only thing it'd cost us would be a dollar a day for a campsite."

Now they felt better. As long as we could run down there from Vermont any time and apparently make money on the trip, they could wait. Besides, since their first spurt of enthusiasm had been absorbed in practicalities, home looked more attractive than ever.

CHAPTER TWO

Under One Roof

NOW THAT Vermont was really our goal, the miles could hardly slip by fast enough. We had thought earlier about stopping at Montreal on our way through, but decided the city deserved far better than a hasty visit. Even my natural history observations, until now taken faithfully throughout the trip, turned into mere jotted notes. Three days and two campsites after that spot in Minnesota, we entered the gorge of the New Haven River. Beyond the gorge's upper end lay the little village of Lincoln, and home.

Now we saw our little valley in a new light. Those great boulders in the streambed, many of them larger than an automobile, were like nothing we'd seen since leaving the West. The steep sides of the valley, with spruces, firs and maples lining their banks, were like Rocky Mountain ravines in miniature. And the tumbling rapids, even though chastened by August's dryness, were a marked contrast to the meandering rivers of the Midwest.

At last we turned into the narrow road that went past our home. It followed every bend of the river, coursing through the little mountain meadows where the crickets and grasshoppers buzzed out their serenades. On our left the land rose gently to the crest of the Green Mountains, the backbone of Vermont, some three miles away. On our right lay the river in its gravelly little valley. A few feet beyond the river the terrain rose more sharply, covered with alders and willows. Finally it ascended to the birches, maples and evergreens of the ridge, a quarter-mile away, which indicated the western boundary of our hundred acres.

Almost in surprise I noted that our old farmhouse seemed to be the same as we'd left it two months ago. Its white clapboards and black roof showed on the bank above the shrubbery along the river. The faded red barn, once the proud home of a dozen fine cattle a generation before we'd moved in, looked as cozily shabby as ever.

I turned up onto the old wooden bridge which spans the New Haven River. Savoring the familiar creak and rumble of the planks strung across its iron girders, we drove slowly over it. Usually it serves as our doorbell, for the grumbling old structure ends right at our lawn. Its sound causes Jack, our old shepherd dog, to rise and welcome the visitors. This time, however, Jack was still staying with some friends, so the bridge spoke only to an empty house.

Well, almost empty. There was a crate on our front porch. And in the crate was a very unhappy hawk.

We looked at the note attached to the crate: "Dear Ron. Heard you were coming home today. Knowing how much you like birds and animals, I'm leaving you this hawk. Will call up tomorrow to make sure you got it okay. G. L."

But who the dickens was "G. L."? Peg looked at the piercing yellow eyes that surveyed us from between the slats of the crate. "I don't know," she said. "Maybe it means 'Good Luck.' Meantime, can it wait while we unload four kids and two grownups?"

Allowing her to propel me back to the car, I considered our latest visitor. Actually I wasn't surprised. I've found myself running a clinic for almost every conceivable critter ever since I won a little notoriety as a second-grader with a learned discourse on why centipedes are classified as insects. (My achievement was the more surprising because—as I learned that same day—centipedes are not insects at all: they're Chilopods, with just too many legs to fit into the insects' six-legged mold.)

The note carried no suggestion to the effect that G. L. hoped I wanted the hawk. No idea as to where the hawk had come from, either. Still, we were used to this sort of thing. I remember one time a woman fifteen miles away called me up and practically demanded that I get a baby woodchuck out of her cellar, as if I had somehow put it there.

So, after we'd unloaded a few of the important things, I turned my attention to the hawk. She was a full-grown marsh hawk, colored somewhat like a sparrow, but the size of a chicken. Her eyes snapped at me, but one wing drooped, exposing the white rump which is the mark of this magnificent bird in the field. At this point, however, her feathers were matted, and the white rump was soiled.

Although her wing was not broken she'd been pretty badly roughed up. Perhaps she had been hit by a car. Peg sized it up more correctly. "Most likely somebody shot her. And ten to one you'll never see G. L. again—whoever *he* is."

She was right on both counts. When we had time later, I put on a pair of heavy leather gloves and took the hawk carefully out to inspect her. She clutched my wrist tightly with one set of yellow talons, and kept those eyes fixed on my face. But otherwise she offered no resistance—a fact which, from long years of experience with animals, I've learned to expect in such a case. Wild creatures can "read" our intentions full well. I have released two skunks from traps, treated a wounded porcupine, and nursed a stiletto-beaked loon after it had become soaked in oil. And I came out of all four encounters without the least bit of bodily harm.

Alison, with her love of animals, usually takes care of feeding and watering our patients. In this case, though, we didn't know what the hawk's diet should be. In the wild, the bird would soar on her two-foot pinions over marshes and swamps, looking for rodents and an occasional small bird. Of course such fare was out of the question now.

We decided to try a chunk of beef. After we'd transferred her to a larger cage, I put a piece of meat on the end of a stick and poked it in at her. She gazed intently at me for a few moments. Then, hopping over to the meat, she pinned it to the floor with her claws. Tearing off chunks with her beak, she wolfed them down.

She was so famished that we didn't give her all she'd take for fear she might overeat. Leaving her to preen herself as best she could at the rear of the cage, we pondered what to do with her.

To keep any wild creature captive was against our principles. We far preferred to "collect" birds, plants and animals by learning as much as we could about them in their natural setting, thus making them our own while leaving them for others to enjoy. Besides, hawks have finally been put under the protection of the law after years of almost universal slaughter. And any animal given legal protection must not be restrained or caged in any way.

So there we were, breaking the law every second, due no doubt to the actions of my unknown friend. Like many of the hunters who roam our countryside almost every day of the year, he'd taken the very sight of a large bird on the wing as a threat to the wild creatures around them. Thank heaven he'd brought his wounded quarry where someone would care for her.

We decided to put her in an old outbuilding, hoping that inactivity would help her wing to heal. We fixed up a low perch in the little milkhouse that stands beside the barn. Then I placed her on the perch. Alison left a pan of water and a bit of food for her.

"Now," said Peg gently to the hawk as we closed the door, "make your wing get better and soon you'll be free."

But freedom came to her faster than any of us had anticipated. The next morning when I went out to look at her, she was sitting on the floor. As I entered the door, those golden eyes with the jet-black centers opened briefly. They looked as fierce as ever, but she was obviously much weaker. And when I returned an hour later to look at her, her eyes had closed forever.

We dug a hole for her not far from where some of our other creatures have been buried, and I just hoped the children wouldn't consider too carefully the fact that she was a female. Most likely, by mid-August, her brood had flown anyway, but possibly not; perhaps, if they needed food, her mate was caring for them. Yet as we tamped down the earth over her grave we knew that somewhere a little bit of marsh was going to miss her.

Just as unfortunate, in their way, as the animals that have come to me because "I didn't know what it was, so I shot it," are the little ones that have been taken from their parents. I've had people bring me everything from half-grown mice to speckled fawns. The story is usually the same: the animal or bird was found, presumably orphaned, all by itself. Yielding to a wonderful—but mistaken—impulse to be helpful, the person who finds the orphan takes it home. He tries to care for it a short time, but seldom has much luck. Finally, when he loses interest or the animal is weakened from improper care, it is brought to me.

I point out that probably the youngster's parents were watching even as it was being "rescued." And I have taken many of them back and seen them reunited with their own kind. If, however, they are really lost, we adopt them into our family for a while, feeding them but allowing them free run of our hundred acres of woods and fields. Our dog Jack has learned to get along with them, too—patiently enduring the attention of baby woodchucks, raccoons, muskrats, blue jays and even a porcupine.

People are often surprised that we don't cage our creatures. Aside from being illegal, however, such confinement is unnecessary. They become dependent on us after a day or so, and never try to cross the river in front of the house or venture into the woods beyond the fields in back. Only as they grow older do our wild youngsters dare the unknown area beyond our lawns and shrubbery and huge maples. In the end, with self-sufficient maturity, they make the break themselves.

To our way of thinking, this is far better than trying to make a pet of some native animal or bird. In all our dealings with wild creatures we keep in mind that they *are* wild, and not merely some cute little plaything. Of course all of us get emotionally attached to certain of our visitors, especially if we've had to nurse them from infancy or shelter them in the house for a while. Nevertheless, even such prized visitors as Pokey, the infant porcupine orphaned by a forest fire—and brought to us with his tiny quills singed and his feet burned—eventually go back to the woods when they get the urge. We never try to stop them.

For us the only animals that can be merely pets are cats and dogs. We don't believe in keeping a creature against its will just for the sake of having it. Since we're fond of the wild birds, we don't have any cats. Thus our only bona fide pet is about sixty pounds of shepherd dog which thumps its tail when you speak the name "Jack." Beauty, our placid old Morgan horse, came to us as a working member of the family while she still had a few years of jogging along country roads left in her. ChiChi arrived a year later as a companion to Beauty. All the rest of the animals are merely transients, and we allow them to return to a life of usefulness in the wild according to nature's rules.

This, of course, is quite different from what so often happens: some bird or animal is raised in a cage until it's grown. Then its owner takes it out to the country to "give it its freedom"—and it meets almost certain starvation, or death at the hands of the first human it encounters.

If wild creatures sometimes pose a problem for us, our domestic animals can give us headaches, too. A typical crisis occurred just the day after we got home. We had been so preoccupied with the hawk that we hadn't paid any attention to the rest of the farm. Now, as Peg and I went to take a look at the blueberry bushes and inspect the woeful job the weeds had done in the garden, the children went out to greet our two placid old mares.

Soon they came back from the fields. One glance at their faces told us something was wrong.

"Dad," said Janice, "where would the horses be if they weren't here?"

I had a sinking feeling even while I suggested calmly that they might be down in the pasture hollow where she couldn't see them.

Janice shook her head. "No. We ran all the way out to the hollow. They aren't there. In fact, they aren't anywhere."

When we'd started on our trip across the country in June, Peg and I both had a little question in our minds as to whether the mares would be all right until mid-August with nobody to care for them; therefore we'd asked Martyn and Vivian Hutchins if they would look in on the farm once a week. Now I got Martyn on the telephone.

His answer didn't help. They had seen the horses two days ago,

17

but hadn't been over to look around the farm since then.

It was up to us to find them. Our property is shaped roughly like an "L," with the foot of the letter in the form of some fifty acres of fields running along the river, and the upright stem being a long stretch of woods running back up the hill for nearly a mile. Fletcher Brown's land fits above and into the angle of the "L," and Dan Garland's woods are along its left side. To the right of the letter is a tangle of blackberries and overgrown brushland belonging to Alec Revell.

A quick telephone check with our three neighbors drew three blanks. Nobody had seen our horses. I called Donald Brown at the general store. His establishment is a bulletin board where all the town's news—and most of the town's suspicions—get aired in a running commentary all day. But not a thing from Donald, either. Nor from any of the customers who happened to be in the store.

So we started out on our horse-hunt. Peg and Janice each took a rope. Tom carried an extra halter in case one of the mares had lost hers during the two months we'd been away. Alison and Roger shared a bucket of grain between them. I loaded my pockets with apples, our mares' favorite tidbits.

It wasn't hard to find where they'd started from. Horses usually respect fences pretty well; even a piece of string across a pathway will turn them back if they see it in time. Now, though, this quirk of equine behavior had apparently been our undoing. Knowing how they'd keep clear of anything resembling a fence, we'd been lax in keeping impregnable the barbed wire which edged our meadows. A casual strand had kept them in check for ten years and somehow we assumed it would do the job forever.

Yet something—perhaps a thunderstorm or a backfire from one of the farm trucks that rattle down the little road—had spooked the horses while we were gone. Or possibly one of them had panicked when her foot caught in a piece of barbed wire half-covered by brush and grass. No matter what the cause, the effect was plainly evident: wire, fenceposts, even bits of shrubs, lay stretched up into the woods, dragged there by what was probably a badly frightened horse.

Several of the barbs had little tufts of white hair caught in them. I winced at each new discovery. This was ChiChi's hair. If the wire had whipped around her leg as she ran, she was likely to have received a nasty gash. And, knowing horses, we figured that the more the wire had cut, the faster our little pinto had run.

We speeded our steps while we dreaded what we'd find. The wire led up into the woods for about a hundred feet. Then a trailing fencepost had caught at the base of a sugar maple. The rusty wire had snapped and ChiChi had gone on, probably giving herself a new case of tetanus at every jump.

We followed the track for a few hundred feet more. Now, thank heaven, we could see that the horses had slowed down. However, this brought up a new problem. Up to this point, the path made by the frightened animals bore some resemblance to the swath made by a small-sized bulldozer. Now that they'd calmed down a bit, their route was harder to follow. Deep-struck hoofprints in the moist humus were easy to track, even for a novice; here we had come to a section where a growth of ferns covered the forest floor. Deer walk through those ferns; so do porcupines and skunks, and each of these left its trail, too. We had to check beneath a likely trace through the greenery in order to see what kind of track could be found.

Of course the horses hadn't made it any easier. They had split up, one headed straight up the slope toward Fletcher Brown's sugarhouse in the woods, the other angled off toward the spruces at our upper corner. We knew they'd rejoin, but to be on the safe side we decided to follow both trails.

Away we went then, like native beaters on a lion-hunt. Peg took Janice and Tom to the left, while I took the younger two with me toward the sugarhouse. The three of us had some of the grain in the bucket, while the other three had the rest of it in a tin pan. Since the horses had been trained to come when we hit the grain dish with a stick, we clattered our way up through the woods, banging and calling our missing steeds.

At least, I started out by thinking of them as steeds. The longer we pushed through the woods with our noisemakers on that sweaty August afternoon, though, the less steedy they became. Gradually they turned into plain horses. Then critters.

And finally, when we broke out into Fletcher Brown's fields, there were the nags, both of them. Ears pricked up, wisps of Fletcher's best timothy hay hanging from their mouths, they looked at us in surprise. Then they looked over toward our left, where Peg and the two oldest children were still banging away in the woods. And neither of those stupid old plugs made the slightest move to come and get some grain.

We called to Peg. In a minute she came out of the woods, too. Now we converged on the horses—who had never seen such a performance before, and wanted no part of it. Wheeling, they galloped off into the Browns' vegetable garden.

We decided on a pincers movement. Peg's platoon went straight up the hill along the edge of the fields. Mine went out and around to get above them from the other side. I hoped Fletcher and Hattie would see us and come out to give a hand. As I considered further, I hoped they wouldn't even be around. Running your horses through the other fellow's garden isn't the best way to cement a friendship.

Apparently the Browns weren't home. After a few well-placed steps in the pumpkins and a nip or two at the raspberries, the horses mercifully departed—of course leaving, for anyone who knew the first thing about horses, signs of exactly where they had been. Kicking their heels like a couple of yearlings, they careened over the fields and back into the woods. By the time we got back down to our own meadows again, still carrying ropes, halter, bucket, grain, pan and apples, they'd made it through the break in the fence and were quietly grazing in the pasture. And I hadn't even thought to pass the apples around while we were coming down through the woods.

Now, naturally, they came right up to us for their grain. Somehow ChiChi had escaped with only a single cut on her leg, but we decided that she should have a tetanus shot, just to be safe. The veterinarian came, washed her wound, put some antiseptic on it, gave her a shot, and charged us ten dollars.

Of course there were other costs. Like half a mile of electric-fence wire, clips and insulators, for instance. Plus a few dozen man-hours (and woman-hours and boy-and-girl-hours) putting up the new fence.

Still, we didn't have to face the potentially biggest cost of all, for Fletcher and Hattie charitably pretended to ignore the whole affair, and remained our good neighbors even if we didn't have good fences.

So here we were, all together again under the same roof—or at least on the same hundred acres. However, as I looked at those ornery horses, I couldn't help hoping that ChiChi had felt the needle just a little bit. Maybe it would teach her a lesson.

CHAPTER THREE

Green Mountain Year

AFTER our abortive woodland roundup, the brown-and-white mare and her chestnut-colored friend had been models of equine behavior. ChiChi limped for a few days, but was well enough in a couple of weeks so Peg and the kids could get in plenty of riding before snow came.

As fall advanced we began to batten down for the winter. With human beings it's a matter of a few storm windows, perhaps, plus a good cleaning for the furnace, or laying in stores of firewood. Overcoats and jackets come out of storage, the car is given snow tires, and an insulating layer of evergreen boughs is piled around the base of the Vermont farmhouse.

For our plant and animal neighbors it's a time of change, too. Up in the woods where we'd chased the horses we occasionally came across snowshoe hares. In summer they would scamper away, their brown coats blending quickly with the leaves and under-brush. Now, with winter approaching, we often saw a hare that was startlingly grizzled. Half its coat would be composed of new white fur, growing in to replace the brown hairs as they fell out. Eventually it would be all white—except for eyes, nose and the black edges of its ears. Its feet, too, would change—developing stiff hairs, or "snowshoes," to allow it to run without sinking into the fluffy whiteness that soon would come to blanket its world for nearly five months.

Our many other woodland friends also changed in their own way. The weasel that we occasionally saw running along the nature trail in the woods likewise donned its winter coat of ermine white. In the deep snow it would be all but invisible: only its beady black eyes and the inky tip of its tail would give it away.

The ruffed grouse put on its cold-weather outfit. Although it maintained the speckled forest-brown it had worn all year, each new winter feather grew in place with a separate downy offshoot at its base. Thus, in effect, our chickenlike forest neighbor developed a suit of winter underwear. At the same time it grew comblike fringes along each toe to serve as snowshoes as it walked through the winter woods.

The white-tailed deer's rusty color changed to a frosty gray-brown. Many of the other wild mammals of Vermont merely donned coats of thicker fur. Some of the animals, like the bear and the woodchuck, stuffed themselves until they were fat as butter. Then they curled up for the winter.

We loved to watch the chipmunks prepare for "the hungry time," as the Indians called it. Poking seeds and wild cherry pits into their cheek pouches until they looked as if they had a whopper of a case of the mumps, they spirited their winter stores underground. It's hard to conceive of a ten-ounce chipmunk doing away with a quart of sunflower seeds daily, but this has happened on our front lawn when one of the little striped creatures has got the urge to collect and I've not been sparing in putting out seeds at the bird feeder.

Sometimes the same seeds will do for two chipmunks. For all their brightness, these little rodents seem to have a mental block when it comes to storing things. One time we watched one 'munk take sunflower seeds to the hollow in the old maple in front of the house—and a second chipmunk remove them as fast as he put them there. Chipmunk Number One kept filling the hole, apparently never tumbling to the fact that Chipmunk Number Two was carefully emptying it.

The beavers along the little streams which feed the New Haven River continued filling their underwater storehouses. Cutting down the poplars, willows and alders along the bank, they nipped off the smaller limbs and floated them down to their pond, where they buried the limbs in the mud. Later, when the land was locked in cold, they could swim beneath the ice to their pantry and feed on fresh twigs and buds as if it were summer. The beaver is one of the few animals that may actually get fat in winter.

Autumn's flaming foliage, of course, was another sign of impending winter. As the leaves go through their last days with a dwindling sap supply, a change in their vital chemistry brings out the reds and yellows which are so much a part of New England in the fall. By shedding its leaves, of course, the tree gets rid of its major source of water loss—and water is hard to come by when the thermometer registers well below zero.

Finally, with many birds gone south, others staying north in their winter garments, and nearly every living thing prepared for winter, we waited for the snow. The first few inches of the white stuff meant sleds and toboggans, but when it got deep enough we would hitch Beauty to the sleigh.

Jingling down the road in the best Christmas-card tradition, we'd meet our share of cars along the way. In a tiny village such as Lincoln, where every automobile is an event, we could usually recognize each car while it was yet far down the road. That station wagon approaching would be Stewart Masterson. The green pickup truck would be Dan and Carrie Chatfield on their semi-weekly trip for groceries. That blue sedan belonged to Selectman Doran Pierce; the rattle around the curve announced that Lee Cassidy was bearing down on us in his farm truck.

So familiar does each car become that we often find ourselves waving to the car instead of to the occupants as it passes on the road. Therefore when somebody suddenly gets a new car, it may take weeks before his old friends learn to recognize him in time to wave as he goes by.

At least this is how it has been up to now. However, with Vermont's burgeoning vacation trade, every fourth car is somebody new, instead of every tenth one or so. Thus, when we're out riding in the sleigh, we perk up just a bit when some unfamiliar car heaves into view. Few of these drivers seem to know how to meet a horse on the road; fewer still know what to do about a sleigh.

Of course, the point is to drive slowly past and keep well to your side of the road if you're meeting a horse. And no automobile horns.

That's the way it's supposed to be. But, like as not, a car from "down country" (Vermontese for that slightly alien land beyond the Green Mountain State) will roar by without slowing. Worse still, and no doubt with the best intentions, it will give a companionable toot on the horn just as it drives by. I once saw a car do this down in our neighboring town of Bristol. The horse took right off up over the roadbank, while its rider contemplated the scene from the ditch.

There's another reason to perk up when you're in a sleigh, though. These quaint vehicles lend a charm to the snow-covered landscape. Alison's sleigh is painted bright red and shiny black. This, with the backdrop of nearby Mount Abraham, Vermont's fifth highest peak, is an irresistible subject for anybody with a camera. So we find cars slowing down and lenses poking out into the winter air at us.

As a photographer myself, I'm glad to help anyone get a picture. In fact, on the few occasions the children have got me into the sleigh, I've insisted that we all wear good colorful clothing.

Sometimes, however, it's hard to resist a sneaky little urge to play the part of the timeless Vermonter when my photographers stop to chat. When they strike up a conversation, I may throw in a generous interlacing of "ayeh" and "down the road a piece" and maybe a few more arresting bits as well. Or it's fun to go completely laconic and squint at the sky as if expecting a repeat of the blizzard of '88. I've often considered taking up tobacco-chewing, too. The juice should make a wonderful photographic contrast against the snow—especially with a movie camera.

Peg doesn't like to ride with me on such occasions. She says she feels like crowning me one. We both know that the Vermonter doesn't slaughter the English language any more than the Virginian does—or the New Yorker or the Californian, for that matter. But if it makes a tourist's day complete, I'm delighted to oblige. However, I'm beginning to wonder about some of the quaint expressions *I've* heard when I've been a tourist myself.

With the passing of the Vermont winter, we enter the delightful time known as mud season. This is a period when it's not really winter and not yet spring, either. The ground, frozen for months, is reluctant to give up its frost. Each boulder and clod of exposed earth, warmed by the sun's rays, becomes a little radiator, melting a tiny circle of snow around itself. The water thus formed flows along beneath the rest of the snow. It collects in little pools and thaws the earth to a depth of a few inches. At night it freezes again, only to repeat the process the next day.

If this were all there was to it, it would be merely inconvenient. Usually, though, Lincoln's gravel roads become rutty quagmires. And what affects us personally is the obvious fact that all the new water must find somewhere to go.

There's a brook that comes down through the woods and flows behind our barn. That is, it's a brook in spring and fall. In summer it's only a trickle. But in that particular mud season, when the deep snows of the woodland gave up their water, it was a racing, foaming flood. And those two benighted mares had seen fit to get themselves stranded in the meadow beyond the waters. This, too, would have been small cause for concern except for one thing: the barn and all its hay were on this side of the brook.

Thus we had to cross about fifty feet of torrent, either with the hay or with the horses. Tom and I decided on the latter.

Tom had a pair of hip boots for the occasion. All I had, however, were knee-length rubber pacs. As it turned out, Tom was no better off than I was. The meadow was flooded only knee-deep, but the water was so murky that we couldn't see clearly to jump across the main channel. So by the time we reached the far side we were both soaked, as the Vermonter says, "up to the crotch."

We hung a couple of ropes around the necks of the mares and started back. But whoever composed that old maxim about being able to lead a horse to water and not making him drink was only half right: we couldn't even lead them to water.

While the rest of the family called to them and threw delicious bits of hay into the air for them to see, Tom and I spoke words of great courage to Beauty and ChiChi. We led them around in circles to get their minds off their troubles. Then we confidently headed back for the barn as if fording a flood was something we did every day. But as soon as we approached the water's edge, they'd plant those horseshoes in the soggy soil and stand there as if they were fashioned in terra cotta by a master sculptor.

Finally we gave up and made our way back through the icy water. I mumbled something about horse murder, but Peg merely indicated two bales of hay which she had thoughtfully carried out from the barn. By now my son and I were numb anyway, so we each staggered back to the horses with forty pounds of timothy. Then we staggered into the house and a couple of hot baths.

That night the temperature dropped well below freezing. The next morning the chastened stream was back in its banks. The horses easily jumped across when the kids called them to breakfast. They spent the next few days in the vicinity of the barn. And if anybody thought the remains of those two bales looked funny sitting 'way out there in the meadow, they wisely refrained from saying so.

Even mud season must pass, however, and the gentle spring came at last. With it came the final portion of the school year, the summer-school bulletins from the colleges, and advertisements from some of the campgrounds we'd visited.

There were term papers to finish, too. Janice had one for history and Alison had one for social studies.

We sometimes read aloud to each other at supper. So when Janice finished her paper she brought it to the table one evening. So did Alison. While it was nothing unusual that the two of them should finish at the same time, it was more of a surprise when Tom and Roger said that they had something, too. As far as I knew, neither one of them had any papers to write.

But when Janice read the title of her history theme, I began to understand. Waiting dramatically until all was quiet, she cleared her throat.

" 'Chincoteague,' " she began, " 'Its History and Geography . . .' "

It was almost the first time anybody had mentioned the little island town since Beauty and ChiChi had pulled their own little rodeo up in the woods nearly ten months earlier. I had assumed that the whole business about going down there had been forgotten, but of course it had merely been smoldering.

Now it burst into flames. " 'Chincoteague,' " read Alison when it was her turn, " 'Its People and Government.' "

Tom came up with "Chincoteague—Its Plants and Animals." And, naturally, Roger capped it off with "Chincoteague—Its Wild Ponies."

They had pieced together quite a story. Apparently nobody really knows how the ponies got there. They are surrounded by mystery. Roger told of a legend that says they're descendants of horses on a Spanish galleon bound for the New World; the ship was wrecked by a storm and the horses swam ashore. Another story has it that they might have been brought over by Columbus. Or they could be the remnants of herds destined for the first settlers in the Jamestown area.

At any rate there they are, wandering wild. They live their lives on a vegetated sand bar which fronts on the Atlantic Ocean. This sand bar, known as Assateague, stretches south thirty-three miles from Ocean City, Maryland. Most of the ponies are concentrated around the southern tip, where Assateague acts as a huge natural breakwater for the smaller island of Chincoteague and its famous oyster grounds.

Usually Assateague is able to withstand the force of Atlantic gales. Sometimes, however, a hurricane roars in and piles the waves so hard against the island that the water is driven far inshore. Then the ponies and other wildlife must seek shelter on higher ground.

But high ground on a sand dune is only a few feet above sea level. Many of the valiant little creatures choose the wrong spot or take alarm only after escape has been cut off. Then, as the rise of the tide adds to the force of the water, they must swim for their lives.

Some of them never make it. Occasionally, when a bad storm has subsided, pathetic little bodies may wash ashore on Chincoteague. And the Chincoteaguers, cleaning up their own débris, know there are more carcasses caught in scrub pines or mired in swamps on the outer island.

Living on rough swamp grass and browsing like deer on shrubs, the ponies have had to eke out a rugged existence. The weak and sickly have been weeded out until the survivors are remarkably tough and wiry. They have probably become smaller, too, and thus better able to find shelter in the low vegetation. In reality, they are considered to be small horses rather than large ponies.

There have been many instances of shipwrecked horses. The Outer Banks of North Carolina, often called the Graveyard of the Atlantic, have had their share. So have other coasts of the world— islands near Great Britain, for example, and in the Pacific.

Many of these wild horses have disappeared as their island homes were appropriated by man in the name of progress. The denizens of Assateague, with miles of uninhabited reef to roam, have been more lucky. Their nearest human neighbors, the oystermen, practically live their lives in boats and have little use for horses. The herd therefore has flourished, and today there are about two hundred ponies—give or take a few, for they are hard to count.

Although a fisherman doesn't need a horse, there are other people who would like to own one of these tough little creatures with their romantic background. So once a year over the last century the herd has been rounded up, a few of the young ones sold, and the remainder and the breeding stock have been returned to their home.

For the past forty years this annual "pony-penning" has been done by the Chincoteague fire department, usually on the last Wednesday and Thursday of July. The horses are rounded up on

Assateague. Thus captured, they become the property of the firemen. Then they're made to swim the channel—mares, stallions, foals and all. The herd spends a few hours in a large corral, and the next day the foals are auctioned off in what has been publicized as the East's Oldest Wild West Show.

It was during this pony swim, according to Marguerite Henry's story, that a little filly nearly drowned. When she was rescued she became the Misty whose adventures we had watched on the screen in Minnesota the summer before.

"Well?" said Janice after they'd finished. "Doesn't it sound like a wonderful place?"

I was about to say something, but Peg spoke up. "It sure does, Janice. And now your father and I have something to read, too."

I was puzzled for a moment, but then she handed me the letter we'd received from Dick and Freda King a few days before, and which she had quietly fetched while the children were reading their papers. Skimming through it, I came to the part on the last page:

". . . So why don't you visit Raleigh this year? Dick has to be at the college all summer, so we'll be right here. After all, we haven't seen you for five years."

Alison's eyes were wide. "Raleigh, *North Carolina?*"

Peg nodded, smiling.

Roger was puzzled: What had that to do with Chincoteague? Janice looked at Roger from the height of a senior in high school. "North Carolina," she said, " is *near* Chincoteague."

Roger turned to me. "Gosh. Are we going, Dad?"

"To Raleigh, yes," I said.

"And to Chincoteague?"

I told him it would be possible to swing around to see the island on our way down to the Kings'.

"Gosh—maybe we'll see a pony!"

For the rest of the evening we talked about the trip.

Roger's enthusiasm was catching, and we happily checked distances and probable stopovers on a map. Even though our trip was yet two months away we started making a list of things to take.

Later that night, when things had quieted down, I happened to notice that Peg was smiling.

"Now what on earth's eating you?" I asked

"Oh," she said, "I was just thinking. Our kids are all growing up, but we aren't getting any older—are we, dear?"

CHAPTER FOUR

Ready, Get Set—

As it turned out, Tom and Janice weren't going to be able to go with us, as both had summer jobs. Roger and Alison, however, were eagerly anticipating the trip, and marked the days off on our large kitchen calendar.

Meanwhile we had decided to stay at Chincoteague long enough to see the famous pony swim, and each of us looked forward to our stopover there for a different reason. The children, of course, wanted to see ponies "like Misty." Peg was anxious for a chance to swim in the surf. And I'd be happy just for a few hours of beachcombing, maybe a day's fishing, and the chance to study firsthand the famed wildlife refuge on Assateague.

First, though, there were a few chores to take care of around the place. Peg and I had made a list of things that needed doing. Then we checked them off one by one.

We'd been making a nature trail up through the woods. It wound for about a mile through the beeches and maples and firs, ending in a little spot where we hoped to have a pond some day. This trail had to be given a spring cleanup so that the underbrush would not reclaim it before we got back to work on it later in the summer. Then there was the hay. Beauty and ChiChi would graze down the new growth in the north pasture, but the south meadow would need cutting before we left.

We had to find somebody to take care of Jack, too. Our clumsy old shepherd dog was so much a part of the family that we felt guilty even talking about the trip in his presence.

And of course there was the little business of money. The kids would bring the contents of their piggy banks, adding up to about ten dollars each. Peg and I counted the coins in the E-Z-Save bank that a salesman had given us. The bank was supposed to serve as a repository for all the fuel dollars we would save if we bought his aluminum siding. However, as we didn't purchase the siding, we hadn't saved much from our fuel money. So it provided about twenty dollars.

So much for pin money. Luckily, I'd just sold a couple of magazine articles and for once the income hadn't all been spent before it had been deposited in the bank. There was enough to see us through, I figured. Nevertheless Peg was going to ask the school to send her salary check directly to the bank. "Then," she smiled at Alison, "we'll know it's there just in case our trip costs more than a dollar a day."

And so the remaining weeks passed. Neighbors helped us cut

and bale the hay. We spent an afternoon clearing brush out of the nature trail. Bob and Betty Douglas promised they'd babysit Jack if we'd leave him off at their house. The postmaster said he'd hold our mail until we got back. Martyn and Vivian Hutchins told us they'd keep an eye on the place again to see if Beauty and ChiChi were all right. We hoped the horses would stay in the pasture this time.

At last it was time to pack. Each of us had a suitcase started; now we set out to complete the job. Roger groaned as Peg took a double handful of adventure books out from beneath his socks and pajamas, and he grimaced as she replaced the books with his Sunday suit, neatly pressed and folded. But he grinned as he saw me take down the fishing poles from the wall and pick up the tackle box.

Alison, noting the whole affair, quietly went to her own room. Although she said nothing, we soon noticed on her table a huge pile of paperbacks that hadn't been there a short while before.

Relenting a little, we set a limit of six books each, if they'd fit into the luggage after all the necessities were packed. Besides, we figured that the King children probably had plenty of swappable reading matter for our homeward journey.

Gradually the pile by the side of the microbus increased in size. We'd taken the middle seat out for more room, and had put the car-top carrier on for good measure. Things like fishing tackle, crab net, my collecting equipment and Roger's little blue surfboard went up on top, while the things we'd be using every day were stowed inside.

Peg and I have learned—mostly the hard way—just what things we want on camping trips and what things we should leave home. For instance, she had once given me a sharp little camp hatchet— which we took with us on just one trip. It is nice for trimming little limbs off trees and for blazing trails, I suppose, but you can't use it to drive a tent stake in anything but sand. It's so small that you can only use it one-handed—which, as a fellow camper admitted between puffs as he nibbled away at a fallen log, "is wonderful exercise, but a helluvaway to cut any wood." So we take a full-sized axe and whack away at tent pegs and firewood to our hearts' content.

The same thing goes for those little folding shovels. Give me something I can get two hands on, and put my back into. One time we had just set our tent up in Indiana when a cloudburst hit us. I worked frantically with that pointed little shovel, trying to dig a ditch around the tent.

By halfway around one side of the tent, I'd had all I could take. I straightened up and flung the offending object as far as I could. Then I stalked into the tent. At that point I was sorely tempted to call a spade something other than a spade. The next day we got a full-sized shovel, and we've taken it camping ever since.

We also put plenty of plastic bags in the VW. We carry these in several sizes. They're useful for all kinds of odd jobs—keeping things wet, keeping things dry, or keeping the two extremes apart. They're fine for soggy swim suits and towels; they make good containers for dirty laundry; they keep the dust off my camera and notebooks, and retain the moisture in the soil around some little plant we may have dug by the side of the road.

Peg can use a plastic bag for a rain hat in a pinch, while just a few feet from my desk is a piece of Arizona adobe wrapped in plastic—as dry as the day we picked it up, five years ago. It would soon crumble to meaningless earth in our moist Green Mountain climate.

We take paper bags and boxes instead of picnic baskets. Then, in an emergency, we always have tinder for a fire. And when the box is empty we can throw it in the trash can or squeeze it to fit a smaller space.

We always tuck in plenty of rope, too. This time our "rope"

was actually a number of yards of baling twine from the horses' hay. It would be handy for a number of uses, including emergency tinder if we needed it for a fire. And those big kitchen matches are better than book matches, by the way. If you're careful, they light and stay lit.

As for kitchen utensils, we prefer pots that will nest one inside the other, with the largest big enough for a dishpan. We'd rather have tin plates and cups than plastic ones; you can heat a metal dish over the fire or keep it warm for someone who's late to meals. Metal flatware is better than plastic, too; we're never in such a hurry while camping that we can't take time to wash dishes. And it's frustrating to have a plastic spoon or fork break in the middle of a meal.

Peg likes the amenities of home enough to make sure that we include a lawn rake and kitchen broom. The lawn rake is handy for clearing a spot for the tent. It's surprising how impertinent a pebble or twig can become after you've lain on it for a couple of hours, even through the canvas floor of the tent, the thickness of a sleeping bag and maybe an extra blanket beneath you as an apology for a mattress. The broom, of course, keeps sand and dirt out of the tent. We've shortened the handle so it will fit in the corners under the sloping roof.

We hardly go anywhere without binoculars. These are handy in two or three ways. Not only are they good for distance viewing, but they're also fine for real close-ups. Try looking through the wrong end of a pair of binoculars at something just an inch away: you'll find that it is magnified tremendously. So there's your hand lens in case you want to examine an insect or a flower at close range.

Another use for binoculars is as a telephoto lens. Focus your binoculars on some distant object. Then steady them right against a tree, say, or the side of a building. Set your camera for infinity and snap the picture through one of the eyepieces. You'll get a passable "close-up" shot that's magnified according to the strength of your binoculars.

We always take our field guides, too. These are the little pocket-sized books that help you identify birds, frogs, minerals, insects—in fact almost anything, if you have the right guide.

It's amazing how much more meaningful a bird or flower becomes if you can give it a name. Roger Tory Peterson's celebrated *Field Guide to the Birds* is fine for beginner and old hand alike. There are also other books in the same and similar series.

One of our favorite pastimes is identifying mushrooms. Here the field guides are extremely valuable. Once you've learned a few old friends among these strange fungi, you can recognize them over the wide geographic range that most mushrooms have. Then, when you find the right kind, help yourself and put on the skillet.

Of course you have to learn to tell them from what the average person calls a "toadstool"—an unwholesome mushroom. As one old-timer once said, "How do you tell a toadstool from a mushroom? Simple. Just eat a mushroom. Then, if it makes you sick, it wasn't."

Although we have almost a fetish against taking any of the living things we see along the way, there are a number of exceptions. I remember one time we were driving along the shore of Lake Erie when the mayflies were emerging. They came in such swarms that they covered everything, clogging the car radiator, clinging so densely to barbed-wire fences that the strands looked as if they were made of rope, and even making the road slippery with their bodies.

Under such a circumstance, I knew it would make no difference if I gathered a few for my insect collection. And, another time in Oregon, there were so many slugs on the sidewalk that their slimy molluscan bodies made treading on the flat surface dangerous. So I collected around a dozen—and we walked on the grass.

On these occasions I either pop a few specimens into a jar of plain rubbing alcohol, which makes a fine preservation fluid, or I use a homemade killing jar. This consists merely of a wad of paper toweling dampened with carbon tetrachloride or cleaning fluid placed in the bottom of an airtight jar with a wide mouth. A disc of cardboard keeps the specimen from touching the moist toweling. A few minutes in the jar is all it takes for a quick and easy death for the insect.

Plants are easy to collect, too. If a plant is plentiful we try to get it all—roots, stems, top. Otherwise we merely take a cluster of leaves or a blossom. We place our specimens in newspaper between two-foot-square pieces of plywood so the whole thing will stay flat. If we have several specimens we use plenty of paper to absorb plant juices.

In all collecting, it's important to note each date, habitat (e.g., lakeshore, rocky ledge, etc.) and area location. Exact identification can come later.

However, if you're not sure of a plant or creature, it's best not to collect it anyway. One time I was taking a friend up along our nature trail. As we rounded a bend where I hoped to show him our only specimen of the wild orchid known as the showy lady-slipper, the motion of a bird in the trees caught my eye. Standing stock still, I searched the branches. After a moment, my friend spoke.

"Ron," he said, "look what I picked. It was just ahead of us in the trail."

And there in his hand was my prize flower.

Unfortunate incidents like this have led us to do our "collecting" by committing to memory the various features of a plant or animal, rather than taking it with us.

Finally collecting equipment, shovels and sleeping bags, tent and tarpaulin were all packed and fitted into place. Having lived

41

through a number of Christmas mornings when eager little voices woke us long before daylight, I'd laid down the law to the kids before we went to bed. "Remember," I said, "even if we do want a good start, six in the morning is plenty early. So if you wake up, not a peep 'til six. Understand?"

At last every light was out. We had taken Jack down to the Douglases' that morning and the house was strangely quiet without the occasional click of his toenails on the linoleum downstairs. A song sparrow woke once, sang a sleepy note, and dozed off again. Out in front of the house the river whispered and gurgled on its thirty-mile frolic to Lake Champlain. A few feet beyond our window we could hear ChiChi and Beauty grazing at the edge of the pasture.

"Goodbye, you four-legged hayburners," I told the mares in my thoughts. "Tomorrow morning we're off to Raleigh. I'll wave a handkerchief at those Chincoteague ponies for you."

The mares, of course, just kept on grazing. And the last thing I remember was one of them nickering softly to the other as if they were sharing some private little joke. Then I fell asleep.

CHAPTER FIVE

Rest Stop

WE HAD SET our alarm for 6 A.M., and it went off as we were having breakfast. Roger and Alison, to give them credit, had tried their best to be quiet in the dawn hours. However, their elaborate whispers finally penetrated my consciousness. By the time I'd roused myself enough to shush them, Peg was awake, too, so we got up and joined them.

Breakfast was a strange affair. Peg had served leftovers the night before in an attempt to clean out the refrigerator; now we had leftover leftovers. We put everything on the table for one

43

last try: two cold hamburgers, a piece of pie, a scoop of mashed potatoes, celery and radishes, macaroni-and-cheese from three days ago.

After breakfast we took the dejected remains of four or five meals out to the compost heap. Then, after cleaning up, packing last-minute things, shutting off the electricity and walking out to the pasture for a final check on the mares, we piled ourselves into the car.

At 8 A.M., on a hot July Sunday, we actually got under way. That noisy little wooden bridge rumbled a farewell as we crossed it. I was at the wheel, Peg was jotting down the speedometer mileage in her notebook, and Roger and Alison were on the back seat with a paper bag of hay between them, "a present for Misty from our horses, Dad."

When you depart from a small town the size of Lincoln it's really an event. Or when you arrive, for that matter. There's a little weekly newspaper which reports on everybody's actions in the towns of the county—such things as "Mr. and Mrs. Wayne Fuller were in Montpelier on business Thursday"; or "Harold Masterson is in Connecticut where he has employment."

Yet with the post office in full swing and Brown's General Store open every day but Sunday, there's really little news that has to depend on the paper for its dissemination. In the words of one villager, "Everybody knows what everybody's doing; I just like to read the paper to see who got caught at it."

Our preparations for Chincoteague had not gone unnoticed by the *Addison Independent*. A week before our trip it had been duly announced that we were preparing to go. Undoubtedly there'd be a note this week to the effect that we'd really left, and when we returned there'd be another note that we'd made it down and back.

I don't deny that it's a wonderful, wonderful feeling to be among such interested and interesting readers of that little weekly paper. That feeling of importance, of belonging, is so nice compared to the loneliness I've felt while living in the city with its many advantages and its anonymity.

Thus it was that our neighbors, forewarned by The Paper, grinned and waved as we drove through Lincoln—Leon Lafayette coming home from his watchman's job at the bobbin mill; Otto Butterfield, whose eighty-eight years hadn't shortened one step of his morning constitutional; Mary Purinton, puttering around her front yard, her five-foot figure greeted with respect by all the townspeople because, as she says, "half the town once went to school to me."

There were the youngsters, too—the Truax boys, the Rotax children, Earl Tilley, the Lathrops—already out on the lawns or headed for the center of town. Eight o'clock in summer is almost a late hour in the country. The kids waved and shouted as we went by. "So long, Roger!" "Have fun!" "Say Hi to the ponies for me, Alison!"

So, feeling like Marco Polo embarking on a world tour, we waved and tooted and sailed out of Lincoln.

Such an auspicious start boded well for our trip, and indeed it was nearly two hours before the children told us they were hot and thirsty.

"All right," said Peg, "we'll get some ice cubes at the next place we can buy them, and take a rest."

We had discovered the wonders of ice cubes a few years before. They're dandy things for kids—and for the adults, too. They have four separate points in their favor: they're delightfully cooling, they satisfy your thirst, they're something to chew, and, if you sozzle them around in a cup, something to do. When we're on a trip, it's not long before we pick up one of those bags of ready-made cubes from a vending machine. But we keep a pail handy to set it in, for those bags often leak when the ice begins to melt.

Sometimes Peg spells me off on long drives. Usually, however, she's so good at reading maps and taking all sorts of notes on expenses, interesting sights and activities, that she keeps to her role of copilot. Here are a few of her notes on that first day:

"Headed for Raleigh via Chincoteague. Hope to camp at Lake Fairfax [Virginia] tonight. Janice working at Owl's Head Harbor, Tom at the Dog Team. Nice jobs for them, but we'll sure miss them.

"Sign outside restaurant: 'Eat here and diet home.'

"9:20. Ice cubes and rest near Granville [New York].

"10 A.M. Still headed south on Route 22. Half the cars going in other direction are from New York, New Jersey, Pennsylvania. Grass always greener in other fellow's yard. They want to go north; we want to go south.

"Another restaurant sign: 'Stop and eat or we'll both starve.'

"11:45 A.M. Taconic Parkway. Broke out leftover chicken. Forgot salt; no napkins. Wet dishcloth better anyway after eating chicken with fingers.

"2 horses in pasture under tree near little church. Sign on tree: 'Pray for us.'

"Safety sign put up by funeral home: 'Drive carefully. We can wait.' "

And so we made progress down the map. Fitful progress, though, because there was much of interest to see and many little stops to make. A vulture soaring over the countryside in lower New Jersey caused us to pause and peer at him with binoculars. Then, as often happens when we stop, we found other things of interest. A bobwhite quail called from a nearby fencepost while I stalked it with my telephoto lens. Alison chased a lizard. Peg wrote in her notebook: "Beautiful spot by the side of the road. Birds, insects, flowers all around. Sound of bees gathering nectar. We'd miss it all if we just kept driving."

Just before dusk we pulled in at the Lake Fairfax campground, a few miles outside Washington, D. C. The children had hoped to make Chincoteague in one hop. However, we really enjoy traveling too much to squeeze the last mile out of each day. So as long as Washington was more or less on our way, we'd decided to detour for a short look at the nation's capital.

After we'd set up the tent we took a look at our new surroundings. It didn't take long to realize that even our comfortable little umbrella tent was primitive by the standards around us. Although it takes us only about ten minutes to set up camp with everybody performing a given duty—Peg raking the grounds, Roger and me unrolling the tent, Alison driving the stakes, me raising the tent from within by means of the umbrella framework, Peg and Roger hitching the ropes to the stakes—our operation was blundering inefficiency compared to the folding trailer that parked next to us.

These people parked the car, opened the trailer with its two double beds, set up a little screened patio on a special framework, and opened out four lawn chairs and a folding table—all in six unhurried minutes. We know, because Peg timed them.

Yet they were slow compared to the two-wheeled trailers. These required merely a bit of careful backing and jockeying for the best spot, followed by dropping cornerposts so the inhabitants wouldn't get seasick every time someone turned over in bed. And the fastest of all was the converted bus or the pickup truck with the camper body built on: the minute they stopped, they were camping.

Even these four-wheeled, self-propelled gadgets have their drawbacks, though. When we were camping at Yellowstone, we were cautioned not to have anything edible in the tent, because the famous Yellowstone bears would walk right in and help themselves. Before we went to sleep at night we watched the great, lumbering beasts as they made their rounds of the garbage cans and fireplaces of the campgrounds.

One pickup-camper drove in and parked near us after dark.

They'd bought a steak at a nearby market, and proceeded to cook it in their camper; afterward, since they were tired from traveling all day, they just stacked the dishes and tumbled into bed.

At about 1 A.M. they were startled by the sound of splintering glass. Looking at the window, they saw a great paw reaching inside. After feeling around a bit, it withdrew. Then it appeared again. Luckily the window was just a bit too high for the bear to get both paws in at once, or he might have hoisted himself right through the opening.

But the bear could still smell the steak; he decided to try another entrance. Nosing around the back of the camper, he began to sniff and scratch at the door. Probably the delicious odor emanated from around the handle. While the man searched desperately for the cleaver, his wife held on to the door handle to keep the bear from accidentally turning it.

Finally the beast gave up. But the man and his wife and their two girls stayed awake the rest of the night. And we in our flimsy tent slept soundly not seventy-five feet away.

Modern conveniences like motorized bungalows and fold-out campsites have led to a new concept of how to enjoy nature. For instance, although the actual Lake Fairfax was a fine little pond with a sandy beach, there was also a gigantic chlorinated swimming pool. There was a large recreation area, too, with a train ride for the kiddies. Down at the other end of the grounds was a store. We couldn't help comparing all this to a campground we'd used the previous year in the Big Horn Mountains of Wyoming, where our only companion had been a roaring brook. The difference was great indeed.

True, we enjoyed our few minutes' dip in the pool before it closed for the night. And it was nice to be able to go to the store and get a snack. Nevertheless, as we walked slowly back to our camp through what was a veritable little town, I was reminded of similar conditions on a far more lavish scale at some places in

Yosemite, the Grand Canyon, Mt. Rushmore. Everywhere, it seems, the emphasis is more on catering to the well-heeled "camper" than on preserving forever the grandeur of our splendid natural resources. In fact, I'm told that one magnificent geyser at Yellowstone has been stilled forever by the building of a new parking lot. And when we last watched Old Faithful, the scene was ruined by the presence of a helicopter hovering just over its towering white plume.

Peg must have been thinking along the same lines. "I just hope," she said, "that in our zeal for opening the outdoors to all we don't turn it into one big urban countryside."

Still, she *had* timed that folding trailer and its six-minute job of setting-up. I also suspected that the time saved wasn't the only advantage that occurred to my favorite housekeeper.

There was a further advantage, too. Just as I was congratulating myself on our good fortune at sleeping on the earth with nothing but a tent between us and the stars, those same stars disappeared. Lightning, which had been flickering on the horizon all evening, suddenly grew in intensity. Now we could hear the rumble of thunder. And before I could drive in a few extra tent stakes and tighten all the ropes, a great blast of wind almost tore those ropes from my hand.

There was a roar over the fields like that of a distant train. But it didn't stay distant; soon it was translated into huge blobs of rain. More wind, more rain—and the storm was upon us.

I'd dug a ditch around the tent to carry off a moderate stream of water. It did nothing for this deluge. In less than a minute the first trickle came in around the tent flap.

I shouted to Roger to move his sleeping bag, trying to make myself heard above the drumming of rain on the tent. When he went to move it, the canvas floor of the tent went "squish." "We'd better all get up!" I yelled. "There's water under the tent!"

So we stood there in the dark, sleeping bags draped over our shoulders, hoping the rain would die down.

By the time the storm finally subsided the floor was ruined. Wherever we stepped, the pressure left a damp footprint. The only thing we could do was to wait for a lull between gusts, dash into the microbus, and spend the rest of the night there.

In the morning the tent was a sight. The wind and rain had buffeted it so much that it drooped and held a great pool where there was supposed to be a sloping roof. We tightened it up until the top half was reasonably drained, and then turned the whole works upside-down to wipe off the bottom. After this I tied it down, spread-eagle fashion, on the car-top carrier where the rush of air would soon dry it.

The crowning touch, however, came as we were packing our soggy clothes. "That was some thunderstorm last night, wasn't it?" I asked an early rising neighbor as he brought some garbage out of his folding trailer and put it in the trash barrel.

"Yep," he agreed. "Sure was. Couldn't get a thing on my portable television."

But there was one segment of the Virginia population that had been delighted by the rain. They were still out exulting when we got under way. These were the frogs, toads, salamanders, snails, earthworms and box turtles which had been biding their time for just such an occasion. As we drove through the early morning mists it took all my concentration to avoid running over some of them. Many had met their fate already, and the road was dotted with pathetic little carcasses.

The turtles would lumber around for a few hours looking for a meal of fruit, snails or insects before things dried off enough to send them back beneath a sheltering stump. The earthworms, brought to the surface by the drumming of the rain, would poke through plant débris, sampling the decaying vegetation before they, too, went below. Snails and salamanders were busy finding tender plants and insects, respectively. Frogs and toads, piping brave little notes as if this were the spring breeding season, hopped everywhere and leaped at anything that moved.

And above it all the birds were singing as if they, too, had had a rebirth. Cardinals, bobwhite quail, catbirds, robins, Carolina wrens, mockingbirds serenaded our progress as we headed again for our destination.

The pervading dampness of clothing, equipment and spirits had brought about a change of plans. We decided to postpone our Washington sightseeing, since we could do it just as easily when returning north from Raleigh. Besides, none of us felt like braving that morning rush hour into the city after half a night's sleep. Nevertheless, as the sun strengthened, so did our spirits, and by the time we'd crossed over to the Del-Mar-Va peninsula our rainy nightmare was almost forgotten.

There was little left from now on but to watch the road signs and urge the car onward. Alison spotted the first advertisement for the island town—a huge poster that showed a curvaceous bathing beauty poised high in the sky, apparently in the middle of a dive. Then we came to more signs—leaping marlin, heeling sailboats, and finally, what the children had been seeking—a dramatic plywood effigy of a wildly bucking horse. There was no question about it: Chincoteague lay just ahead.

In honor of the occasion we broke out an early lunch of bread and ham and chocolate milk and ate as we drove along. Scarcely had we finished than the long, low tidal marshes began to appear on either side of the road.

Each moment the marshes became more open. The roadway narrowed until it resembled a series of bridges built on little hummocks of land. Then the road arched up over a channel. And there at last, with its neat little houses, its fishing vessels and—hidden somewhere—its horses, lay the little town of Chincoteague.

I slowed the car on the bridge to take in the scene. Beneath us roared a square-ended, sloping-bottomed boat propelled over the water by a powerful motor. This was our first view of what I learned was a "Chincoteague scow," the sturdy, homely little boats with such a shallow draft that they can negotiate the few inches of water that cover the mud flats at low tide. "I suppose," one Chincoteaguer solemnly assured me later, "we'd use them on Main Street after a rain if they didn't need an automobile license."

Roger was looking through the binoculars. Suddenly he laughed. "What's that sign mean, Dad: 'Private—Keep Off.' Keep off what? The water?"

We looked to where he was pointing. The sign in question stuck up out of the water. We decided it referred to that portion of the mud flats immediately surrounding it. Oyster beds, probably. I was beginning to like Chincoteague. Peg could have her beach and the kids could have their horses. I'd find my own mud flat and go on a king-sized oyster binge.

We continued across the bridge and on to Chincoteague's main street. The town was a bustle of activity.

An unhurried old resident in an antiquated car stopped to chat with a friend who was walking on the sidewalk; at once an impatient tourist in the car behind him leaned on the horn. A startling girl in skin-tight pants came out of a store wearing a brand-new cowboy hat. It looked identical to some I'd seen in New Mexico imprinted with the legend CARLSBAD CAVERNS. This one, though, had CHINCOTEAGUE.

Slowly we drove past the stores, the restaurants, the hotel. Then Alison let out a whoop that made me slam on the brakes. I thought that at least we had hit an occupied baby carriage.

She pointed ecstatically across the street. "A horse! A real Chincoteague pony!"

Now it was Roger's turn to join in. "And there's another! And two more! The town's full of them!"

With the kids leaning out of the windows and exclaiming at every new horse, we thought we must be making quite a spectacle. But nobody seemed to notice. I guess when you're zany over horses, it's almost as bad as being an ardent fisherman.

Suddenly the din from the back seat doubled in volume. "Misty!" cried Roger. "It says you can see Misty at the Beebe Ranch—down this street and turn left!"

With our children in such a state that I feared they would expire from apoplexy, we drove into the yard of the valiant little pony's home. We paid the price of admission, took in the little bag of Vermont hay, and soon were standing in the presence of the little movie heroine herself.

I am not much at describing horses, but I had to admit the little horse was one of the most striking creatures I'd ever seen. Her golden color, long flowing white mane, and gentle manner couldn't help but endear her even to me. If you can use the word "charming" in connection with a horse, she was it. If not, supply whatever adjective means the same thing and can be more properly used in equestrian circles.

The children talked in hushed tones. When we finally pried them loose from their idol they were—with no play on words intended—misty-eyed. From that point on, nothing could have gone wrong with our trip. We could have had that rainstorm all over again. A tidal wave could have washed us right off the road. A tornado could have snatched our tent and its occupants from the campground. Mosquitoes could have landed two deep all over us. Nothing would have mattered. They had seen Misty.

With their clamor hushed for the time being, I was able to drive without interruption to the municipal campground. There, surprisingly enough, we found things almost deserted. All those people downtown, and hardly anybody at the campground: I couldn't understand it. Still, it gave us the choice of sites, one near a tree and handy to the sanitary facilities.

Backing our VW into place, I picked out the exact spot for the tent. "We'll park the wagon there," I said as we hauled the tent out and set it up, "and then it'll serve as shelter and shade. We can eat between the wagon and the side of the tent when we want to."

Which, as it turned out, just went to prove how much I had to learn about Chincoteague toward the end of July.

CHAPTER SIX

Buggy Ride

A FRIEND had written ahead to introduce us to Warren Conant, Chincoteague's postmaster. Somehow I'd always thought of postmasters as people with green eyeshades and ink on their fingers, and their heads full of government regulations. Warren wasn't a bit like that. When we presented ourselves to him later that Monday afternoon, his friendly grin and joking manner put us at our ease at once.

Learning in the letter of my interest in natural history, he had arranged a surprise for us. The following day, he said, we were invited for a ride in a sand buggy around the Chincoteague National Wildlife Refuge. In this way we could view firsthand the preserve on the outer island of Assateague, where the ponies lived.

We were curious about the emptiness of the campground when only two days remained before the pony swim, but Warren assured us that we had merely been earlier than most of the campers. By the end of the evening we realized how right he was. The influx of humanity began with a big bus from Tennessee, loaded with Girl Scouts, and followed by a station wagon with their luggage. They drove around the place for a few minutes and then decided to share the other side of the tree with us.

Looking over the vast camping area, I remarked to Peg that their nestling so close was like two strangers taking adjacent seats in an empty theater. The driver and the Scout leader knew what they were doing, though. They just took a good spot while it was available.

Good spots weren't available long. It was as if everybody had been waiting in line and someone had just opened the gates. Cars, trailers, converted camper-buses began to arrive. Soon a pall of dust rose above the little grassy road which enters the camp. We went to bed to the shouts of children, the sound of tent pegs being driven, the smell of hot dogs, bacon and coffee. And we wakened in the morning to find that a little blue trailer had staked a claim to part of what we had formerly thought of as "our" driveway.

"I see you're not lonesome," Warren Conant said as he arrived to take us to the headquarters of the wildlife refuge. Before leaving us in the care of the officials, he introduced us around as "Ronald Rood, the wildlife writer, and his family" until I felt at least like Ernest Thompson Seton.

Our sand buggy was a Jeeplike pickup truck with oversized, low-pressure tires that allowed it to jounce over the dunes where an ordinary vehicle would flounder hopelessly. With Alison and Roger in the open back of the buggy and Peg and me beside the driver in the cab, we crossed the bridge connecting Chincoteague with the island of Assateague. We were now in the refuge, and on the home ground of the wild ponies at last.

A shout from the children announced the first ones. "Stop!" cried Roger as he spied about a dozen animals grazing on a marshy meadow. But hardly had we come to a halt than both children shouted in unison: "Go—*go!*"

I looked back at them in surprise. They were wildly flailing their arms about their heads. Hordes of mosquitoes had risen from the marsh grass, and were attacking them with a viciousness we could almost hear. In another instant the comparative sanctuary of the cab was invaded, too.

We started up again and drove slowly parallel to the herd. We could see three or four foals with the mares, while a stallion stood apart from the rest. He was solid chestnut, but his mares were almost any color a horse could be. They ranged from uniform brown through piebald to silver gray. One of the foals looked as if it had been caught broadside with a bucket of white paint.

The mosquitoes were bothering them, too, for they stamped and swished their tails. This was a new trial of existence for the little foals that we hadn't even considered.

"Are those ponies really wild?" Roger called in disbelief.

For answer our driver swung down a little grassy trail. It led in the general direction of the stallion and his family. As we got closer they raised their heads and looked at us. Finally the stallion snorted. Then, whirling, he herded his little band at a run toward the deeper grass.

"They're not all this spooky, by any means," our guide admitted. "Sometimes they'll let you get up real close. But they're wild, all right. There's a prize for anybody who can stay aboard one of 'em for three minutes at the roundup."

We saw more of the little bands. Then we set out to see the island itself.

57

It was one of the strangest rides I've ever had. That vehicle could go anywhere. We careened up the island by means of an old trail. Every so often we'd meet a few "gumboot cowboys." These were Chincoteague men who usually wore gumboots—rubber fishing boots—but who were now dressed to ride their full-sized horses for the business of rounding up ponies. Most of the herd had already been driven into a large corral to await the swim to Chincoteague the next morning. Then mares, foals and stallions would make the crossing just as their forebears had done once each summer during the past century.

As we met the successive groups of riders, we would inform them of bands of ponies we'd seen. "Oh, John's after those," they'd tell us. Or perhaps two or three of them would guide their horses off in the direction we indicated.

It was fun, being in on the start of pony-penning this way. But this was just one of the island's many attractions. The pines, mid-Atlantic hardwoods, and low shrubs that cover the sandy soil contained myriads of living creatures.

As our buggy advanced it was preceded by an active little vanguard. Grasshoppers by the thousands leaped out of the way until they reminded us of popping corn. Some were green, and would have been invisible the instant they arrived at their new spot except for the violent swaying of the green grass caused by their landing. Dune grasshoppers, pepper-gray like their surroundings, surprised us whenever an apparent bit of sand launched itself into the air. Longhorned 'hoppers, relying on their streamlined camouflage, merely swung around to the back side of a grass blade. There they'd wave those long feelers at us as we drove by.

Other insects flew out of the way; some of them were even swift enough to run. These latter were the tiger beetles, iridescent jewels of blue, or green stripes, or rainbow colors. Half flying, half running, these fierce armored warriors, nearly an inch long, could catch almost any other insect their own size in a lightning attack. Now they scampered ahead for a short distance until we were too close, then darted effortlessly aside.

We came to a sandy area that was full of little pits that looked as if there had been an air raid with marbles. Since the mosquitoes were not bad here in the open, we stopped to examine the pits more closely. They were perhaps an inch deep and an inch and a half in diameter.

While we watched, a spotted tiger beetle accidentally tumbled down into one of them. Instantly there was a snap at the bottom of the pit and the tiger beetle began to struggle violently. He bit at the sand with his scimitar-jaws, but to no avail. With each passing second he sank deeper into the sand until at last he disappeared from sight. He had stepped into the jaws of a creature every bit as implacable as he was—the ant lion, or "doodlebug."

We dug into one of the pits and exhumed its squat little inhabitant. About the size, shape and color of a pumpkin seed, the ant lion lay motionless for a moment, its jaws opened almost to a 180-degree angle. Then, in a series of jerky rowing movements with its stiff projecting legs, accompanied by a peculiar hunching of its body, it backed into the sand and out of sight. Soon, by throwing sand grains in the air as it backed in a decreasing circle, it would make another new little pit and be ready to resume its patient waiting game.

Looking around, we discovered other creatures—the eaters and the eaten in the desperate little world of the dunes and marshes. A wolf spider, her hairy body the size of a marble, trundled her egg sac along behind her like a bundle of washing as she stalked a millipede. Suddenly, with a rush, she pounced. On impact, however, her prey curled up its segmented body, offering her only an impregnable coat of mail.

Another wolf spider, represented by a little pile of remains, had come to its end at the teeth of a mouse or shrew. The runways of these little mammals were everywhere, providing a lacework of tracks across the trail and holes beneath the grass, sedges and rushes.

Holes of another kind dotted the bank of a tidal inlet. Each of these, varying around an inch in diameter, was the home of one of America's oddest individualists—the fiddler crab.

This mudbank crustacean gets its name from the huge, unwieldy claw of the male. One claw is small, like both those of the female, but the other may be nearly as large as the rest of the creature's body. Holding it in front of him, he draws it back and forth as if playing a violin.

Apparently the reason for such an appendage is to excite the female to a state of uncontrollable desire, for, as the biologists' old saying goes, "The fiddler crab waves his huge claw in the air as if to say 'Wilt thou?'—and, like as not, she wilts."

Obviously the ruse is crowned with success. Not only were there hundreds of holes, but sometimes it would seem as if the whole bank was in motion as a regiment of crabs scuttled out of the way as we walked.

We saw these fascinating citizens of the island sand bar, plus many more. Once we spotted two Sika deer from our sand buggy. These small Asiatic animals were privately imported and released years ago, and have found the coastal wilderness to their liking. We saw the tracks of skunks and foxes, too.

And we saw birds. Birds by the hundreds and birds by the thousands. Water birds, shore birds, song birds. Plovers, sandpipers, ducks and geese flocked to the sky in clouds as we raced along. Warblers, catbirds and mourning doves flew from the branches. Gulls, terns and skimmers sailed overhead. Herons and bitterns stalked through the marshes or flapped away in alarm as we came too close.

Not until we had gone several miles up the island did our buggy lurch to a halt. Then, turning toward the ocean, we came to the barrier dune. This vital mound of sand, stretching parallel to the coast, keeps the ocean's fury from overrunning the island, and cuts the bite of the wind. Built by the forces of wind and water, it is forever shifting and changing.

After a storm the dune may have been picked up by the wild waves and moved inland; or it may have been severed at a weak point, allowing the running sea to flood through the breach. Therefore in many places it is strengthened by lengths of slatted fencing—like the snow fences of colder climates—erected to catch the wind and make it deposit its sand. In other places it has been stabilized by plantings of sea oats, beach grass, and salt-tolerant shrubs.

Our buggy climbed the barrier dune. There we paused. To our north and south, as far as we could see in either direction, stretched some of the finest unspoiled coast left on this continent. As with so many other wonderful areas, it had long been threatened by thoughtless developers who saw little more than the possibility of profits. It was still being threatened as we looked at it. However, I am happy to report that, at this writing, it has been saved from extinction: recently it became the Assateague National Seashore Area. So for once man has acted wisely before it was too late.

Carefully crossing at a place where the fence was nearly hidden by the mounting sand, we drove down on to the beach. Then, turning south, we started for home along the shore, the waves of the open Atlantic Ocean pounding to our left.

Now there were even more birds. Sandpipers, gulls, terns flew up ahead of us and settled down after we had passed. Thus we drove almost constantly beneath a wheeling, screaming canopy.

The pointing hand of our driver directed our eyes out to sea. Scores of porpoises played several hundred feet offshore, their backs gleaming in the sun as they rose from the waves. Occasionally they would break clear of the water and fall with a great splash.

Almost immediately he told us to look ahead. High up on the sand, where it had been carried by the tide, lay the carcass of a whale. Clouds of birds rose from it as we approached. Keeping to windward as best we could, we slowly circled the decaying mass. It wasn't large as whales go, I suppose; perhaps thirty feet long, perhaps less. But it made the children's day complete. From then on, the bodies of rays and harmless sharks scarcely attracted their notice: they'd seen a real live—or rather a real dead—whale.

The tour ended at the public beach area on the lower end of Assateague, where Warren was to pick us up in his car. Now, with the naturalist made happy, the swimmers came into their own.

The frothing blue-green combers were delightful. As we joined the other bathers at the edge of the surf and fought each successive wave, I suddenly felt something stir beneath my toes. Even though all the sand on the sea bottom was in motion, somehow this felt different.

Seized with a thought, I reached down and scooped up a handful of the sand. There was my little tickler, plus a dozen of his relatives. The sand bug, *Hippa talpoides,* is admirably suited for its wild life in the zone of the crashing waves. Streamlined to the size and shape of a large olive, this sand-colored relative of the crabs finds a unique existence where other creatures would be dashed to pieces.

With each wave the small crustacean tumbles out of the fluid sand and spreads feathery appendages into the water. These serve as strainers for the myriads of tiny organisms which share its tumultuous world. Then, as the wave retreats, Hippa tucks in its net, flails out with little paddles, and buries itself in the sand to await the next onrush of water.

My single handful of sand had scooped up several sizes of the creatures. Behind me, at the edge of the waves, were flocks of sanderlings, picking up these and other crustaceans one by one.

The sanderling, a kind of sandpiper, is my favorite bird. It is as well attuned to the surge of the waves as its tough-shelled quarry. Flying up the beach ahead of each watery invasion, the flocks alight as soon as the wave comes to a stop. Turning, they follow it down, straight little beaks jabbing in the sand like the needles of sewing machines. Their dark legs twinkle as they run to keep up with the water before their food has burrowed out of reach. Up with the next wave, back down with it as it retreats—and so, on and on.

The universal food of the sea is so plentiful, and the sanderling is so perfectly fitted for its life, that this bird may be found wherever the sea crashes on sandy beaches—which means, of course, all over the world. As I stood, captivated, on that Virginia shore, I realized that I might be sharing my delight in the gray-speckled beachcomber with someone else ten thousand miles away.

My pleasure in this thought was suddenly interrupted. "Porpoises!" called a bather. As I looked seaward toward a band of the creatures lazing perhaps five hundred feet offshore, several of the swimmers, apparently on impulse, started out toward them, followed by Peg, Roger and Alison. I dashed for my camera kit lying up on the sand and, while the swimmers tried to get close to them, I took telephoto pictures of the proceedings.

The porpoises—or, more correctly, dolphins, for a porpoise is one particular kind of dolphin (with the game fish called "dolphin" not any relation at all)—were secure in their position as among the swiftest things in the ocean. They paid little attention to the clumsy humans except to give a flip of their powerful tails and torpedo far out of reach when a swimmer came too near.

Before long I put my camera away and swam out to join the others. We could hear the dolphins sigh and breathe as they surfaced. The effect, although strange, was not in the least unpleasant. Somehow we felt a kinship with these great mammals. Such a feeling, I am sure, would be completely missing if one were to swim in the presence of large fish.

Probably it was foolhardy to swim so far out into waters we didn't know. However, if there had been sharks, the dolphins would have kept them away. Sharks keep their distance from a school of dolphins rather than chance injury and even death from being rammed in concerted attacks launched by these otherwise peaceable creatures.

Sea stories abound with tales of dolphins which have befriended shipwrecked sailors and even nudged them to safety on shore. I recalled the way that wild animals have often been able to sense the good intentions of humans. Besides, thinking back on it now, perhaps we swam without fear among these intelligent denizens because *we* sensed *their* good intentions.

That swim was second only to the whale as the children recounted our day's adventures to Warren and Pauline Conant at supper.

"It sure makes pony-penning pretty tame," he said to his wife with a wink. "And after a ride in a sand buggy, there's no use suggesting we go to the carnival tonight."

But of course he allowed himself to be won over by the children's protests. Before we went to the carnival, though, he took us for a drive around town. As we rode, he told us of the carnival's tremendous success.

The roundup of the ponies had been going on for more than a century. At first this was all there was to it: the capture of horses by a few men, and sorting out good animals for sale. Then, around 1925, the Chincoteague firemen got hold of the idea. The atmosphere of the roundup demanded a carnival, they figured. So they set up thrill rides, games of chance, souvenir stands, and they engaged folk-singers and variety shows to hold the crowds.

They capitalized on another outstanding local asset, too. This is the famed Chincoteague oyster, which thrives in the shallow waters surrounding the island and is eaten all year round. Scooped from the sea and rushed to booths at the carnival, these delicious bivalves are the main ingredient of something called an oyster sandwich—impossibly gooey as such a thing may sound.

Actually the oysters are mixed in a batter and fried to a golden brown, like a pancake. They go like hotcakes, too—and for good reason, as we discovered later when we sampled them. The tang of the sea is in each sizzling bite, and I'm sure many a doubter has been converted to a seafood lover with the first taste.

With their two-week carnival, which features those oyster sandwiches and is climaxed by the wild-pony roundup, the Chincoteague firemen have enjoyed a whopping success. This we discovered as we drove past the firehouse.

No, I should capitalize it: Firehouse. It is a two-story building perhaps fifty feet deep with an eighty-foot frontage along the main street. I had driven past it earlier, when, at a hasty glance, I had thought it was the high school. Now two of its five great doors were open to reveal gleaming engines ready to roar away if so much as a match dared to get out of hand on the island.

There's always a waiting list for membership in the Chincoteague Volunteer Fire Department. Mentally comparing it with our struggling counterpart back home in Lincoln, I was duly impressed. And if Chincoteague's fire insurance rates aren't the lowest in the nation, they should be. This town of about two thousand people, surrounded by water, has adequate fire protection. Excuse me again: Adequate Fire Protection.

The gumboot cowboys we had seen on Assateague were part of that fire department, and the next two days would see the results of their work—the pony swim and the auction of more than half a hundred foals at more than half a hundred dollars each; with the proceeds going to fatten the treasury of the C.V.F.D.

The carnival lived up to its publicity and was still roaring when we said goodnight to Warren and Pauline and headed back to camp. They promised to meet us early in the morning for the pony swim, which was to be not far from our tent.

Cars were still arriving at the campground, their lights shining redly in the dust. I wondered where all the people would find places to sleep. In fact, I was almost surprised to see that our tent was still standing, and unoccupied.

Out in the parking lot there were cars from California, Maine and Florida. Some cars, probably, were there only for the night; but at least a few of them must have come hundreds of miles, as we had, to witness the happenings of the next two days.

Near us were trailers darkened and still. There were trailers housing parties in full swing. There were tents with people playing cards, or people reading by the light from gasoline lanterns. One man was just returning another's hammer; he'd been using it to drive the stakes for his tent. Babies were crying, children were laughing, mothers were calling their youngsters to bed. A gray-haired woman was playing a musical saw while a man accompanied her on the harmonica. Teenagers walked along with transistor radios blaring. Not far away one newly established campsite had a six-inch-high picket fence with a miniature gate bearing the legend THE SMALLS.

We listened to the soft harmonizing of our Girl Scout neighbors as we got ready for bed. And, as we finally zipped ourselves into our sleeping bags, I had to admit it: for a little fellow, the Chincoteague pony certainly had tremendous pulling power.

CHAPTER SEVEN

Auction

WE MADE IT to our front-row seats at about eight o'clock in the morning, and we weren't any too early. Even though the swim wasn't scheduled until about 11:30, many of the choicest spots along the low beach were already taken. The rising tide of the ocean, advancing on the shore, was met by a descending tide of humanity, crowding toward it.

The firstcomers spread their blankets out on the grass and prepared for a few hours of reading, sunbathing or sleeping while they waited for the big event. Soon the press of the crowd obliged them to fold up their blankets; before long, with people standing in front of them, they, too, were forced to stand.

On the water a veritable flotilla was assembling. Craft of every description waited at anchor or sped back and forth, venting their masters' excitement. There were rowboats, cabin cruisers, open speedboats, sailboats, dinghies, and not a few yachts.

Occasionally we could read the names of the home ports painted on the boats: Darien, Cape Cod, New London, Norfolk, Tampa, Staten Island. A large Coast Guard craft, bull horn blaring and crew smartly uniformed, kept the boats out of a lane between us and the tip of Assateague, some eighth of a mile away. It was through this lane, when the time came, that the ponies would make their swim.

Warren had wangled a position for us on the boat of a friend. We hoped to have an uninterrupted view, out on the water like that, but the population explosion on shore soon spread to the water. It seemed as if every one of the island town's hundreds of boats had been commandeered for the day. Our little craft had to maneuver this way and that so we could see and take pictures.

I asked our skipper how many people there were on the quarter-mile of beach. "They'll keep coming for another hour," he said. "Usually something over twenty thousand by the time everybody gets here."

I looked at the boats, which in some cases were anchored so closely together that they touched, and I had a mental picture of the ponies crossing by stepping from one boat to another, as if on a pontoon bridge.

Warren's friend grinned at my notion. "It's better to swim 'em across at ebb tide when the water's slack and low. But low tide comes at the wrong time of day right now. So they're going to swim 'em when the tide has come in full—just before it turns and starts out again. That way they won't have to fight any current."

With our binoculars we could make out the ponies, grazing on the opposite shore. They looked peaceful and unconcerned at all the commotion on their behalf. Once in a while two stallions would rise above the rest, pawing and biting as family groups came too close together. Around the outskirts of the herd the gumboot cowboys rode easily or sat and chatted, waiting for the signal to close in.

The marker buoys, anchored along the main channel between our shore and Assateague, had been slanting with the force of the incoming tide. They straightened with each passing minute. The anchored boats, which had all swung to point into the current, drifted more lazily. The crest was only minutes away.

Suddenly, from the other shore, there was a report like that of a pistol. Instantly the riders leaped into action. Shouting, whistling, slapping their thighs, they bore down on the pony herd. The wild horses wheeled in confusion. Then they started for the only path that lay open to them—that eighth-mile strip of water.

Crowded at the edge, they neighed and whinnied. We could see a splash here and there as a horse slipped and stepped into the water. It seemed as if the foals would be crushed in the press of scores of running, pushing bodies. But still they clung to the familiar land.

Then one plunged in. Then another, and another. The riders plunged in, too, urging them on. With a turmoil of spray, the shouts of riders and the slap of leather reins on the water, some two hundred horses leaped into the sea.

Now the whistling and shouting stopped. The riders turned back to land. Silently they looked after the departing herd. From the crowd around us rose a murmur of excitement. It gained in intensity as the horses drew closer.

From the horses themselves came a sound I can never adequately describe. Part of the sound was the calls of the mares to their little ones, answered by whinnies from the foals. Some of these plucky youngsters swam with their chins on their mothers' rumps to help keep their heads out of water. The over-all sound also contained the commanding cries of the stallions as they urged their families forward. And, as they finally gained the shore, there was the snort and neigh of triumph as each pony felt solid ground beneath its feet.

One spotted foal, smaller than most, lost touch with his mother; confused, he drifted away from the herd. The noise of the crowd took on a different sound as we saw his plight. A boat pulled away from the raft of vessels to go to his rescue, but luckily his tiny hoofs soon touched bottom and he struggled ashore unassisted.

Later we learned that he wasn't the only one who'd had trouble. The firemen had found a tiny foal who had been born more recently than the others. She was so small, in fact, that they didn't even try to swim her across the channel, but brought her over separately in a skiff.

As the herd rose from the water, the people melted away before them. More mounted riders appeared and took command. Without giving the ponies a chance to catch their breath and disperse, the riders urged them onward, guiding them to the big corral. And, as if driven by mounted riders ourselves, the thousands of us followed.

Here at last we could get close to the wild ponies. Safe inside the corral, they were no longer pestered by the riders. Mares licked the wet coats of their foals. Stallions nipped and whirled as they assembled their family groups. The youngsters, tuckered out from the exertion, lay down wherever the mood hit them. Amazingly, I never saw a single one get stepped on.

We were surprised at the size of the adult ponies. They were larger than we'd realized—about the size of the cow ponies we'd seen in the West. Clean-limbed and graceful, most of them looked quite capable of carrying a man. The foals were perhaps the size of a German shepherd dog, with long, gangly legs.

Peg and I marveled that such slender limbs could have propelled the foals so surely through the water. We asked one of the firemen about it.

"Nothing to it," he said. "Those little critters can swim from the day they're born. If you ask me, they're half porpoise."

We watched as the commotion in the stockade died down. Most of the Chincoteaguers headed for their homes, as it was now past noon. The rest of us were slower to depart. We could overhear the conversations of people as they appraised the merits of the foals in preparation for the auction on the following day.

"I like that little spotted filly," a woman said to her husband.

"Maybe," he said slowly, "but the little mares will cost more at the auction. Now, you take that chestnut-colored fellow over there. See how straight he stands? Wouldn't the kids love him?"

Other conversations were more businesslike. "I got room for three of those in my horse trailer. Wish I could take four. They sell fast as pets back in Arkansas."

None of this, of course, was lost on Roger and Alison. For the first time they realized what the auction would mean. "Gee, Daddy. You mean they're going to take them right away from their mothers? Won't they miss each other?"

I assured him that the mares would have other youngsters next spring, after the dangers of winter were past. Besides, I figured the present crop would soon be tapering off on their milk diet, so they would shortly be more or less on their own. And, since that vegetated sand bar where they lived could support only a limited number of ponies anyway, "harvesting" the year's increase without cutting into the foundation stock was almost the ideal method of conservation. With no wolves or mountain lions or other natural enemies to hold them in check, they would otherwise increase until disease or starvation cut them down.

My explanation seemed to satisfy the children. After all, those little foals were too appealing, anyway: they couldn't be sent back to the sand dunes where nobody could appreciate them.

Lots of other people seemed to think the same thing, for the rest of the entire day was given up to just about one activity— pony-watching—with lunch and supper merely sandwiches toted around and munched as we gazed at the sights before us. Finally, reluctantly, the four of us went off to bed.

When we awoke, the campground looked as if some strange malady had struck. One after another, families deserted their trailers and tents and headed for the carnival grounds. More than half the campsites were silent by the time we had had a hurried breakfast and taken our own departure.

The foals had been cut out of the herd and stood in a little corral. Then, almost without fanfare, and shortly after we'd shoe-horned ourselves into a place where we'd have a good view, the first foal was put up for auction.

She was taken up a chute from the little corral. Two husky men held her while she thrashed and whinnied and kicked. "All right!" called the auctioneer. "Who'll be the lucky one to get the first colt?"

Someone asked him if it was a mare. "Yep," he said, "this here's a mahr colt. Who'll give eighty dollars to start her a-goin'?"

Someone called out "Fifty!"

"Fifty," repeated the auctioneer. "I've got fifty dollars. Who says fifty-five for this fine little colt?—That's it! Now who'll give sixty? Sixty-five?"

And the auction was on.

One after the other the colts were brought to the block. Some of them struggled and kicked so that it took two men to hold them. Others reacted to their first touch of human hands more quietly. The hoss (male) colts averaged perhaps sixty dollars each. The little mahrs (mares) brought ten or fifteen dollars more.

Early in the bidding that tiny mahr colt who'd been ferried over by the firemen came up for sale. She excited a great deal of interest, and finally went to a family from Massachusetts.

AUCTION

I stood entranced, watching black colts, spotted colts, golden colts all find new owners, new homes. Some were received matter-of-factly by experienced traders. These colts were passed on to handlers who took them to waiting trucks in the hope of resale back home. Others were received with wonder—and sometimes with happy tears—by some delirious child as his parents swapped a few greenbacks for a bill of sale.

And one of these children was Roger.

We hadn't meant to buy a pony. Heaven knows that we had never planned such a thing. Heaven knows we already had two mahrs at home. And heaven knows, too, that we had no truck, no trailer. Just a microbus.

But of course heaven knew a few other things. It knew we had no Chincoteague pony. It knew that my son, whom I love, desperately wanted one. And it also knew that I had tucked a blank check away in my wallet.

It happened shortly after Roger appeared beside me in the crowd. He had his pocketbook in his hand, and in it was the contents of his piggy bank. His hand trembled as he presented me with that flat little purse.

His eyes were wide and beseeching. "Here's all my money, Dad," he said in a voice so low that I had to bend down to hear. "Seven dollars. Could you . . . could you—?"

I looked at my son. His eyes held their look of entreaty even while his countenance prepared itself for disappointment. We had gone over our budget so carefully before the trip that he knew how closely we'd tried to plan everything. Still, he must have hoped, something might turn up in the nick of time.

"Roger," I said, "you're not supposed to buy a pony, just like that." I snapped my fingers. "What will you do with it? We already have Beauty and ChiChi to ride."

"But this would be a pony of my *own*. And I'll pay you back, Dad. Honest."

73

I considered for a moment. But only for a moment. That look on his face cried out for an immediate answer. "All right, Roger," I told him. "I guess maybe we can help you. Pick out the one you like. And you've got to bid on it yourself."

For a moment he was speechless. The thing that had seemed beyond all hope had actually happened. Then as a look of realization came over his face, I suddenly had a realization of my own. Never, never, even if I write a best-seller or fly to the moon, will I have a feeling to equal the one which came to me at that moment. My boy wanted something with all his heart, and he had given me his worldly possessions as a pledge for it. And I was able to help him get it.

Now Roger's ten-year-old face was a study in concentration as he looked carefully at each colt in turn. Finally he made his choice.

"Forty!" he called as a tiny brown colt lunged and struggled without a sound in the arms of a burly fireman. The auctioneer picked up the bid, and someone on the other side of the crowd raised the price.

Most of the other bidding had been silent, with the auctioneer calling out the prices as a bidder raised his hand or gave a slight nod. But Roger, in the excitement of this moment, came through loud and clear. "Fifty!" he cried when it came his turn again.

The other party bid fifty-one. Roger raised it to fifty-two. And so it went up, a dollar at a time, until it rested at fifty-seven. At this, a man beside me spoke up. "Sixty dollars is a nice round figure. Tell the boy to bid sixty and see what happens."

Roger looked at me. Then he squared off and let the crowd have it. "Sixty!" he shouted, loud enough to be heard all over the carnival area.

That three-dollar bid did it. The auctioneer glanced at the opposition, but apparently he saw no sign. Looking back at Roger, he smiled.

"He's yours," he said softly, "for sixty dollars."

AUCTION

With hands that had a hard time keeping steady, I wrote out that check to the Chincoteague Volunteer Fire Department. They in return handed me a receipt for the purchase of "one pony."

Peg had been a short distance away when Roger had called out his first price. During the bidding she came to where I stood, and I gave her what was meant to be a confident grin. After that, although I could feel her looking at me, not once did I take my eyes from the pony or the auctioneer. Alison, who had been sitting on a fence rail near the corral, had come running when she realized who had won the bid.

Well-wishing strangers congratulated us on our choice. Roger, overwhelmed, could do little more than stand with his arms around his pony's neck. He grinned and murmured his thanks and absently patted the little colt while he considered his new station in life as the owner of a Chincoteague pony.

Finally Alison ran back to the car for a rope. We picked up a tiny halter from a vendor who just happened to be near the table where you paid for your ponies. Then, with Peg and myself holding him, Alison and Roger slipped the halter on the pony's nose.

And there we stood. The five of us.

Our little scene was repeated all over the fairgrounds. Anyone who has been to an auction knows how impulsive you can be on occasion. And when it's a gangling little foal three feet tall that's up for bids, anybody can get carried away.

The new owners had all kinds of plans for their charges. "I'm going to brush her four times a day and feed her nothing but grain," exulted one young buyer.

"I'm going to show my Roxy at every horse show in the state," proclaimed another.

"I'm going to race mine."

"Mine is going to be on television."

"Mine'll be in movies *and* television."

Some of the remarks sprang from bewilderment. "Good

heavens! Whatever will my husband say when he finds I bought a pony?"

"It's your fault, Martha! All I said was 'I wonder how the fishing is at Chincoteague?' "

It was surprising to learn of some of the places these ponies would go. Our hundred acres, of course, is not a large farm, and many of the foals were destined for bigger places. On the other hand, from the remarks we heard, not a few of the little creatures had a dubious future:

"Do you suppose my brother will let us keep her on his farm?"

"They'll let us pasture Trigger on the baseball field, Ma. I know they will."

"We can probably keep him in the summer all right. But in the winter—how do you get hay in the middle of Philadelphia?"

"But you *said* we were going to have a little place in the country, didn't you? If not, why did you let me bid?"

After all, it *does* take a piece of land about the size of a baseball field to pasture a pony, and that much again to supply hay for the winter. Ruefully we had to admit that not a few of those ponies, bought so hastily and with so many good intentions, would probably end up as mere curiosities, pets—sort of summer romances that hung around through the winter. Worse still, if they went to homes smaller than our farm, they might become definite liabilities, finally to be sold, or given away to any taker.

The firemen allowed us to put our little hoss colt back in the corral with his mother until the next day. Peg mercifully refrained from upbraiding me for my impulsiveness. She said not a word, either, about the agreement we all lived by: not to "collect" animals or plants, but merely to record them in our memories or on film. This of course should go double for something as rare and unusual as a Chincoteague pony. But then, Roger was *her* son, too. And anyway, as I pointed out, three horses at home couldn't be much more trouble than two.

76

Her only comment came after we had watched our new family member in his corral and had given him a little hay in the hope that he was weaned enough to nibble it. "What color would you say he was?"

"Gosh," I wondered; "I don't know. Maybe it says on the bill of sale." I unfolded the little slip of paper that gave us title to sixty dollars' worth of Virginia wildlife. "The slip says 'mouse brown.' "

She thought for a moment; then, "What do they mean, 'mouse brown'? He's fawn-colored. Like a little fawn."

"Yes," I agreed, as she slipped her hand in mine and we started for the campground. "A fine little Chincoteague fawn."

CHAPTER EIGHT

Aftermath

W ARREN had had some work
at the post office and hadn't been there when we made our purchase. Now I went to break the news.

"Guess what happened this afternoon—" I began.

"You bought a pony."

I stared at him. "How did you know?"

He chuckled. "Don't act so surprised. It happens all the time."

"But now what do we do? How in the dickens do I get a pony
out of here and back to Vermont?"

He considered that one for a while. "There's one fellow with a horse trailer going as far as Baltimore," he offered helpfully. "He said he had room for another pony. And there are any number of truckers around who'd haul your horse to Alaska if you wanted them to."

That wasn't the answer. I told him we were heading on down to Raleigh, and we couldn't send the colt to Vermont all by himself.

We mulled over the problem some more. Then his face, which had gone serious with thought, relaxed. "Well, Ron, you've got no other choice. Take him with you."

I must have looked my amazement.

"Sure. In your station wagon it'll be a cinch."

But a *horse* . . .

"Just a little one, Ron. Tell you what. After supper we'll measure your pony and see if we can't make a little crate for him. Then he can go to Raleigh, too."

Unable to make a better suggestion, I drove back to the carnival grounds where I had left Peg and the kids. Our fawn-colored white elephant was sound asleep in the corner of the corral.

By now the grounds had taken on a different look. Those who had not bought a pony had gone their separate ways. The people who remained were thinning out rapidly, too, as they hastened to get their charges home as soon as possible.

Others besides ourselves were adopting makeshift means with regard to their ponies. One man in a pickup truck with a smooth metal floor started up with a brown-and-white filly in the back. He'd put down a bit of hay to make her footing nonskid, but she still slipped in her struggle to keep her balance as he drove away. Halfway down the road her hoofs made such a clatter that his wife got out and squatted in back with her. The truck had Delaware plates, so they probably didn't have too far to go.

A woman who wasn't so fortunate as we were in having a friend like Warren made room by taking the back seat out of her car and shoving it into the trunk. As she and her four-legged passenger drove away, I wondered how they would make out on their trip back to New Jersey.

I was still bemused as Warren arrived with a tape measure. We took the dimensions of our pony: about thirty inches high, a foot wide, and forty inches long. Leaving the children to watch over him, we went off to an old warehouse to build the crate.

This accomplished and the crate left at the corral to be ready to install in the car, we went back to the campgrounds and an early night's sleep. It had been quite a day.

We were watching the pony and his mother in the corral the next morning when Warren drove up once again. There was one more place he wanted to take us—to his camp out in the middle of Chincoteague Bay. "Pauline and I would like a mess of clams. Want to come along?"

I had treaded in waist-deep water and mud for the round quahaug, or littleneck clam, when I was a boy in Connecticut. The gooey muck had clung around our bare feet as we'd felt with our toes for the clams. Somehow I always expected to run into a crab or maybe an eel, but the hard-shelled molluscs were well worth it. So, as our pony could stay with his mother a few hours longer, we headed for the dock and Warren's Chincoteague scow.

It was another wild ride. The powerful motor kicked up such a fuss and the bay was so shallow that we often churned up mud with the propeller. The boat slapped and pounded and headed for a tiny speck in the middle of the wide expanse of water between Chincoteague and the mainland. As we drew nearer, the speck turned out to be a grassy island, barely above water, surmounted by Warren's tiny shack.

We stopped when we were still some distance from the camp. Jumping over the side and clinging to the boat, we set about treading out our dinner.

You'd think it would be easy to tell the difference between the empty half of a shell and a firm, tightly closed clam; and eventually, I guess, it is. But to such nonexperts as the four Roods every hard object in the muck felt the same. Our toes singled out cockle shells, pieces of horseshoe crab, oyster shell, chunks of waterlogged wood, and, sometimes, those round clams.

There's a knack to treading clams that comes only with practice. Getting the clam in position with the side of your foot, you kick it up to the vicinity of your knee. Simultaneously you reach down and grab it before it falls back to the bottom. Such dexterity, however, was far beyond us, so we had to dip beneath the water for each prize.

This was fine in the warm, murky water until, one time as I ducked below the surface, my face came smack against something soft. And big. And slippery.

I gave a yelp and half jumped into the boat. Everybody but Warren very nearly followed me. But he just chuckled. "Oh, don't let the jellyfish bother you," he said. "Just try to keep clear of them if you can."

I felt I had to save my reputation as a naturalist. "It was just the suddenness of it all," I said. "Besides, some of them sting. Some of them don't."

Peg, of course, couldn't resist. After all, she'd been brought up on Long Island Sound where they often picked up jellyfish and threw them at each other like snowballs. "Oh?" she said. "Tell us what kind the next one is, Ron, won't you?"

We saw a number of the transparent, umbrellalike creatures pulsating their way slowly through the water. Some of them were the size of half a lemon and bluish in color. Others were as big as grapefruit with a purplish tinge. Now and again a red one nearly the size of a half-watermelon drifted by, trailing two-foot-long tentacles in the water. Fish and small organisms, touching those tentacles, would be paralyzed and drawn up under the umbrella for food. But now that we were on the alert for the jelly-fish we could usually see them coming before they were lost in the cloudy water around our feet.

Gradually the pile of clams in the boat increased in size. When we had gathered about a bushel we climbed in and headed for the shack once more.

As we approached the camp, I contemplated it with awe. The tiny structure, made of bits of planking and driftwood, somehow clung together on stilts a few feet above the spongy ground. A fancy barrel-arrangement collected rainwater from the roof; I'm sure Warren could receive national acclaim if he foisted it off as a piece of pop art.

Away from the shack and precariously balanced on more stilts was another startling edifice which the Conants delicately called "the facilities." Its door opened inward so the occupant could en-joy an uninterrupted view of the bay and the distant shore. Or—in sudden emergency—he could slam the door shut. Between the two buildings was a catwalk on more stilts, making you feel that you were walking the plank.

We left the boat to the mercy of the jellyfish and proceeded to our fresh seafood dinner. Along with the clams, there was a basketful of blue crabs Warren had brought, plus a generous sup-ply of those Chincoteague oysters.

The crabs, nearly as colorful as any crustacean that swims, snapped their blue and red claws as Pauline dumped them into the pot. Soon their olive-green tops and varicolored undersides turned a uniform brick red as they quickly succumbed to the live steam. When I was a boy I remember being heartbroken as I saw a lobster boiled. Since then, however, I've learned that it is pos-sible to raise the temperature of the water wherein a crustacean is living so slowly that the creature shows no sign of discomfort. So apparently it makes less difference to the crab than I used to think.

I doubt that I shall ever have a better meal. What more perfect atmosphere for a gourmet luncheon could one ask than the call of the gulls, the gentle slap of waves on a boat, the sweep of the bay and the pervading smell of the salty air? We even had weathered wood paneling, too.

All too soon we had to leave. Packing up the food that remained, we closed the door gently so the place wouldn't fall down. Then we started whacking over the water on our way back to Chincoteague.

When we arrived at the fairgrounds the adult horses had been moved to another corral, and our pony looked tiny and lonesome there by himself. Whinnying, he ran to the fence.

"What shall we call him?" Peg asked.

"Oh, that's easy," said Roger. "His name is Little Fellow."

Scooping the pony up before he could protest, I guessed his weight at about fifty pounds. So his name fitted him perfectly.

We placed his crate in the station wagon and turned to the pony. We were putting off our departure for Carolina until the next day, to let the colt get used to the rope and halter. If he was going to be difficult, we would all be better off struggling with him now than halfway between Chincoteague and Raleigh.

Therefore Alison and Roger took turns leading him around. Or that's what they attempted to do. Little Fellow, though, for all his seeming gentleness and good nature while we had been patting him, was not buying even one strand of that lead rope. He sailed and bucked and shook the kids around until they were airborne half the time. It looked almost as if we would do better by trying to fly him behind us, like a kite.

Still, even though he persisted, so did they. Peg and I stepped in and helped, too. And since there were more of us than of him, we figured we'd be able to outlast him.

After perhaps half an hour, while we stood in a deadlock and puffed at each other, the pony decided to end it. Just like that.

He'd been standing with legs braced, pulling backward; Roger had been doing roughly the same thing at the other end of the rope. Suddenly the pony slacked up—so suddenly, in fact, that Roger staggered and nearly fell.

And from that moment he was Roger's pony. While we watched, amazed, Roger turned his back to him and walked confidently away, still holding the rope. Little Fellow trotted smartly after him, his tiny hoofs making little thuds on the hard-packed soil.

Roger led him a hundred feet away, then turned and started back. With a little whinny of recognition, the pony almost forced Roger into a run as he scampered back to where we were standing.

We of course petted and praised him, and he basked in his glory. He tossed his little mane, switched his tail and stamped his feet. This was fun and he wanted more.

We took turns leading him until the time came to take him to the campground. "We'll do it," volunteered the kids. "You drive back to camp, and we'll see how long it takes us to walk Little Fellow a mile."

Peg and I hopped in the VW and drove away. Just before we turned the corner I glanced at them in the mirror. They were walking along the edge of the paved road. Alison and Roger were on either side with the pony in between. Already they had picked up a friend: a little girl was skipping along with them, too.

We had been back at our tent about half an hour when we became aware of a commotion at the entrance to the campground. Looking down the road, we could see a group of children coming our way. As it drew closer it resolved itself into a flying wedge. At the head of the wedge was the current holder-of-the-rope. Slightly behind him were Roger and Alison. Buried somewhere at the other end of the rope was Little Fellow, surrounded by an adoring mob.

Finally our eyes picked him out. As many children as could

reach him had their hands on his back. And he was living it to the hilt. He arched his neck and bounced along, obviously enjoying his part in the parade.

Roger set the camp children to gathering the lushest grass they could find. Peg and I placed a pan of water for him. Then we stood back to watch him eat and drink.

He sniffed at the grass. When his nose hit the water, he jerked back, startled. His reactions brought up a problem I had been warned about after the auction.

"This one's smaller than most of 'em," a fireman had told me, "so I doubt if he's weaned from his mother very much. You might have to feed him with a bottle for a couple of weeks."

Apparently this was indeed the case. I drove into town and bought a nursing bottle, into which we poured a little warm milk.

By now a crowd of campers had gathered. Children and adults were fascinated. They stroked him and took pictures while Roger girded himself to feed the pony.

When all was in readiness Roger put his left arm around Little Fellow's neck and presented the bottle with his other hand.

The pony wanted none of it.

Bracing himself, Roger took a tighter hold and tried again. The pony merely turned his head and tried to back away. Then Alison tried, and finally Peg. The results were the same.

The campers were full of advice. "Mix sugar with the milk," said one. "They like it better that way."

"Or salt," said another. "Horses love salt."

"Perhaps the milk's too hot," ventured still another.

"I've got some honey back at the trailer. Want to smear some on the nipple so he'll start chewing on it?"

The most immediately helpful suggestion came from an onlooker with a bent for psychology. "Why don't we all go away for a few minutes? Maybe he's bashful."

Whereupon they all retreated to a respectful distance to watch the feeding. But it made no difference. That pony just couldn't seem to understand what we were trying to do.

At last, after nearly an hour, we gave up, discouraged. Roger was close to tears. "Gosh, Dad, he's hungry. But he doesn't know how to eat."

I thought of all the other infant animals we'd had in the past. While milk is a universal food for young animals, it sometimes needs to be made extra palatable to get them started. I've found that a tablespoon of honey or corn syrup to a cup of milk usually works pretty well. If they don't drink it at first, they often learn to if some is smeared on their lips. Yet obviously such a step wasn't necessary at this point. Little Fellow was liberally smeared already. Our struggles had seen to that.

Peg looked at me. "We've tried everything there is to try," she said, as if I held the answer. "Now what do we do?"

All I could venture for the time being was to see if maybe he would finally get so hungry that he'd *have* to eat.

Since we couldn't think of anything else anyway, we decided to leave it at that. Every hour, all afternoon, we kept offering the bottle. And every time it brought the same result: a polite but firm refusal.

I presented the problem to Warren. He, in turn, presented it to a friend of his who had a few horses of her own. "Try a little of this," she said, offering me a pailful of grain. "If he still won't eat, put a little molasses on it."

I put a little grain in a pan and set it down by our pony's water and his heap of grass. After ten minutes of no results, I poured a bit of molasses on the grain. But all he did was tip it over with his foot.

We had had enough animals around our place in Vermont to know that probably he would learn to eat before he starved. However, it was important to have the problem settled just right before we started for Raleigh in the morning. And if he wouldn't eat here on the campground, we figured he'd be that much less likely to eat after he got in the VW wagon.

We'd turned away from him for a moment when we heard one of the camp children yell: "Hey! Your pony's eating!"

Sure enough. He was nibbling at the spilled grain on the ground. A glad cry from Alison made him look up for a moment. "I played hard-to-get long enough," he seemed to say. "Now, if you don't mind, I'm hungry." And he went back to his grain.

So—two hurdles over: he would lead, and he would eat. Now I thought of the little crate in the microbus. One hurdle left to go. Plus, of course, a day's ride to Raleigh. I suggested that we try putting him in his crate just to see how he'd fit, but Peg would have none of it.

"No," she said. "Let's not disturb him as long as he's doing so well." Then she added as an afterthought: "Besides, what if he got scared? Then he'd be twice as hard to put in tomorrow."

After supper we drove the VW up to the side of the tent where the Girl Scouts had been. In preparation for an early start in the morning we packed it with everything except the tent and sleeping bags.

And except, of course, Little Fellow. Our fawn-colored sea horse lay at anchor on his rope just outside the tent. He lulled us to sleep that night with the comforting sound of grass being nibbled and grain being chewed.

CHAPTER NINE

A Pony,
Among Other Things

THE DISTANT SOUND of
hoofs came to our ears as we were folding up the tent the next
morning, and at the same time we saw a number of children running across the campground.

"What's going on?" I called.

"They're swimming the horses back to Assateague," a boy
shouted over his shoulder as he ran past us.

With a quick check of Little Fellow, we broke into a run, too. The horses were being herded back to the water's edge once again. The group was markedly smaller now, with only a few colts left. These were mostly fine little mahr colts which the firemen had reserved as a nucleus for a continuing, vigorous, youthful herd.

Here was another way in which the herd was kept in good condition. Not only had the marketable "crop" been harvested, but also, just as the prudent farmer may save his best corn and his best potatoes for seed, about a dozen of the finest fillies were being returned to their homeland.

Nor was this all. On the rumps of several of the horses were great daubs of pink paint, placed there for easy identification from low-flying aircraft taking part in population studies and disease control programs. Thus Chincoteague cultivates its wild ponies almost as carefully as one might tend the plants in a window box. And since a record is kept of the buyers of each little colt, there's always a known supply of additional breeding stock to draw on if the necessity arises. Once, a few years back, just such a need was filled after a hurricane had battered the island and drowned many of the little band.

At the water's edge there was a scanty crowd of people to see this, the other end of the pony swim. They were mostly Chincoteaguers, plus a few of the campers and tourists, like ourselves.

The horses needed little prompting for their return trip. Ahead of them, across that stretch of water, lay Assateague and freedom. They plunged in, talking and neighing to each other as before. This time, however, there were nowhere near so many high-pitched little whinnies: only a few of the mares had young with them.

We saw the first of the herd gain the other shore. Pulling themselves up on the grassy bank, they shook themselves and formed back into little family groups. Then each group took its way out over the meadows. Soon they fanned out and became smaller in the distance.

I gazed at that distant herd and realized that now our pony's father and mother had returned to that wild island. Doubtless they had already forgotten him. Up to now the band of which he was a part had still been with us. Now, however, they were but specks on a grassy sand dune in the distance—and growing smaller as we watched.

Dropping my eyes to the shore in front of us, I spotted an orange film carton, a reminder of the hordes of people who had thronged this very beach several short days ago. As I watched, a ripple lapped higher than the rest. The film carton shifted a little. With the next wave it bobbed away on the water; soon I could see it no longer. The sea had erased a last vestige of man's feverish activity—and Little Fellow was really ours.

Returning to camp, we packed the last-minute things. Then we took a final look around the grounds. Tent, sleeping bags, kitchen utensils—all stowed. Nothing left except a pony tied to a shade tree.

Here was the moment each of us had secretly been dreading. After all, our little pony had thus far lived his short life in the freedom of sand dunes and sea air. What if he kicked his way loose from the crate when we tried to confine him? What if he broke a window? What if he even broke a leg?

Probably we had all asked ourselves the same questions in our minds. Now they were about to be answered.

"All right," I said casually to Roger, as if it had just occurred to me, "let's have the pony."

Roger walked up to Little Fellow, who gave a little nicker of greeting. He untied the pony and walked him to the car. "Lamb to the slaughter," I said to myself, half wondering just who was about to get slaughtered. The hoofs of a playful colt are amazingly sharp; those of a desperate colt even more so. We wouldn't have room to get out of the way inside that bus if he began to thrash around.

We had built one end of the crate so it could be detached to serve as a loading ramp. Now we laid it in place and let the pony smell it. "See?" I said, as he cautiously looked it over. "Nothing to hurt you at all."

Carefully paying out rope as he went, Roger entered the VW. Its two big side-loading doors were opened, so Little Fellow could still see him inside. "Here," he called, "here's some grain." Then he pulled gently on the rope.

The minute the rope tightend, the pony stiffened. We all started to talk at once in what was calculated to be a reassuring tone. But Little Fellow didn't seem to be reassured. He wouldn't put one foot on that ramp.

"Help him," said Peg. "Give him a little boost."

I cupped one hand behind the pony and put the other under his chest to help urge him forward.

The results were immediate, and they were more than adequate. Little Fellow gave a tremendous leap. Clear over the ramp he sailed, right into his crate. In fact, he leaped so hard that he bumped his nose on the opposite window.

There he stood, sneezing from the bump and looking back as much as to say, "Well, aren't you going to shut the door?"

Hardly daring to believe our good fortune, we tied the end of the crate in place. A number of campers had been watching the whole procedure; now they whistled and cheered as we started the car. With the horn tooting and hands waving from every window, we drove away from our friendly campground for the last time.

We stopped at the post office to say goodbye to Warren and his friends. Little Fellow nickered and tossed his head as if he wondered what all the fuss was about. Then Warren presented his parting gift. It was a small bale of hay.

"Chincoteague hay," he explained. "It'll keep your pony from getting homesick."

Thus fortified, we turned and left the little island town. Down the street and over the bridge which spanned that wonderful bay, past the private oyster grounds, through the salt marshes—four people and a pony, headed now for North Carolina.

We naturally had wondered how our four-footed passenger would make out as a traveler. We needn't have given it a thought: he was as good at automobile-riding as he was at everything else. I don't know if ponies ever get carsick, but ours certainly didn't. Although he had no way to tell us, we felt sure he was enjoying it.

Originally, much of our luggage had been stored between front and rear seats. The folded tent went on the floor, and most everything was piled upon it. However, with Little Fellow in his makeshift stall taking up a greater portion of the center of our vehicle, we had to reshuffle our camp equipment. The tent ended up, an ungainly mass, behind the rear seat. The rest of the equipment had to find lodging wherever it could.

We were relegated to opposite corners of the station wagon as we rode. Roger was tucked directly behind the pony, at the left rear. Alison was at the right rear with luggage piled on the seat between herself and her brother. Peg was on the passenger side of the front seat with more luggage piled between herself and me. As the driver I had more room than anybody.

Almost anybody, that is. Little Fellow couldn't turn around in his stall, but he could stand up or lie down. He could also turn his head back and nuzzle Roger, or turn it forward and do the same to me. Every so often I'd feel the touch of a little tongue or the friendly nibble of a pair of lips on the back of my head as our pony gave me a greeting.

When we stopped to get ice cubes, Alison put a few in a pail for him. Since we figured that he was about six weeks old and had been born in early June, he probably had never seen ice before. Yet he relished the coolness just as much as we did, and licked his cubes until they melted.

He liked ice cream, too. Roger found this out by mistake after we had visited a dairy bar. Roger was resting his hand against the crate, and the new member of the family took a husky swipe at his cone with a well-aimed pink tongue.

Every fifty miles we'd have a pony-stop. Little Fellow learned to back out of the car by means of the ramp, although he always preferred to leap back in. While one of us led him around to nibble grass and stretch his legs, the rest of us cleaned out the newspapers and straw he'd been using as bedding. This way we managed to keep his stall clean and dry. I have often wondered what the highway crews must have thought when they emptied some of the roadside trash barrels and found litter that had obviously once belonged to a horse.

We had lots of fun with our unusual passenger. He was a perfect springboard for jokes. We soon discovered that he would whinny if he saw anyone near the car. This led me to scandalize Peg by driving—quite unintentionally, of course—very slowly past two girls in shorts who were crossing in the middle of a city street. Little Fellow's reaction—and theirs, too—was spontaneous and unrehearsed.

Whenever we paused to let one of us go into a store to buy something, it wouldn't take long for passers-by to discover our unusual passenger. Not wanting to go right to the window and stare, they'd call out to us as we re-entered the car: "What you got there? A big dog?"

"Nope."

"A goat?"

"Nope."

"Aw, come *on*," they'd say. "What is it?"

Usually they didn't believe it was a pony until they had looked closely for themselves. Then, since it usually meant a long conversation if we stopped to explain, we would just smile sweetly and drive away.

Little Fellow didn't like to be left alone in the VW. Often, for our pony-stops, we chose a roadside spot where a car or two was already parked. Then we'd all get out for a moment and leave our little pony. As we sauntered innocently away, a piteous whinny would cleave the air. It was fun to watch the puzzled expressions of the other people as they tried to figure out where the noise of a horse had come from. And, invariably, when they finally discovered his whereabouts, their first question would be the same: "You really got a *horse* in that wagon?"

Everyone who saw him was taken with him. Cars whizzing by when we were exercising him would screech to a halt, back up and discharge their curious passengers. One woman made us promise to wait while she hurried home for her camera. Little Fellow was petted, photographed, and offered grass, sugar lumps, fig bars and even chocolates.

A white-haired man, learning that our pony liked ice cream, went across the street to a little refreshment stand and brought back cones for everybody. Then, while his wife ran the movie camera, he stood in the hot sun and allowed Little Fellow to lick the ice cream until they both were a mess. But a happier old gentleman I have seldom seen.

As we rode along, our pony would often poke his nose out of the window. Most oncoming cars did not notice him, but we could always tell when he had been spotted. The other automobile would indulge in some rather erratic behavior. The car would swerve a bit; then in the rear-view mirror I would see its brake lights flash on for a moment. Afterward the car would continue on its way doubtfully, as if scanning the windows of other automobiles for the sight of more ponies.

Occasionally one would actually stop, make a quick U-turn and come speeding up behind us. It might even follow us for a while, or pull alongside.

Cars going in our same direction, of course, would do this often. It was not unusual, either, to have a car flash by and then slam on its brakes right in front of us while its occupants peered back to confirm what they thought they saw. I don't recall that we caused any wrecks, but we sure went down into North Carolina in the midst of some mighty queer driving.

As we approached Raleigh, the children got to wondering if maybe we shouldn't break it to the Kings gently that we had a pony. "Think we ought to find a telephone and let them know Little Fellow's with us?" asked Alison.

I drew a breath to answer, but Peg spoke first. "Believe me, they'd be more surprised if we didn't have something. Ever since your father showed up with that hairless fox, nothing shocks 'em."

The fox had been one I'd discovered while we were living next to the Kings in Connecticut. Dick was studying for an advanced degree in agricultural economics at the University of Connecticut, while I pursued my master's degree in wildlife management. One winter day while searching for tracks in the snow, I came across the strangest fox I'd ever seen. There was no fur on his legs or sides, and just a few hairs on his back and tail. His skin was all scaly and rough. He blundered into bushes and trees as I approached, and seemed in the last stages of misery.

Warily circling closer, I realized that he was blind: that scaly skin had grown over his eyes. I took off my heavy jacket and managed to maneuver him to where I could throw it over him.

He struggled but was too weak to put up much resistance. Picking him up, I materialized at Freda King's door with my bundle.

At this time we hardly knew the Kings, beyond nodding to them as we drove to college each morning. But Peg and I were both going to be away from home all day, and I hoped Freda could keep an eye on the fox while we were gone. So I asked if I could put him in her garage.

She accepted, no doubt mainly from bewilderment and the desire to help an animal in need. And on this wobbly foundation was built a friendship that had stood for more than fifteen years at the time we were bearing down on them with a pony.

The fox, by the way, did not long survive his ordeal. Too emaciated even to eat, he succumbed the next day. My zoology professor analyzed his trouble as a whopping case of mange— which killed the fox and nearly ruined our budding relationship with Dick and Freda, as well. Every time their cat scratched himself for the next two weeks we felt guilty. Luckily, however, the cat never came down with the disease.

After the fox, we had entertained the Kings with all the other birds and animals which have resided with us. They have always been wonderful about it, too. So we felt no qualms about showing up at their doorstep with a pony. After all, as my Lincoln neighbors say, the tail goes with the hide.

We arrived in Raleigh about dusk. Dick and Freda came out to meet us but, working out a little conspiracy we'd planned, we dashed out and met them halfway. Roger stayed in the car with Little Fellow to keep him quiet, so they'd not know we had a horse.

We gave them some lame explanation about Roger's not being able to make the trip. Then we got them back into the house. Shortly there was a knock on the door.

When they opened the door, there stood Roger and his pony.

"Good grief!" said Dick. "*Now* what have you got?"

Roger grinned. "Well, a pony, among other things."

With that he strode into the room. Little Fellow, taking his cue perfectly, leaped across the threshold and followed him.

The Kings were delighted. They patted and praised him. But at last the question came up.

"What'll we do with him tonight, Dad? He might get lonesome, standing outside all night."

Freda looked at Dick. Dick knitted his brows as if in deep thought. Then, without a word, he brightened and led the way to the garage.

Dispossessing their car, they fixed up a spot for Little Fellow. "Yessir," said Dick, as we re-entered the house, "glad you could make it. Seems like old times."

The next day half the neighborhood managed to come around to see the pony. One boy, a bit smaller than Roger, placed his hand on the pony's sturdy little back. "How would it be if we rode him?" he inquired.

At once Roger was all business. It would be impossible, he explained, until the pony was at least two years old. One of the things that could ruin any horse was to mount him before he'd got his growth.

As he went on outlining all the things that were necessary for the health and welfare of his pony, I was gratified at the amount of horse lore he had managed to accumulate on his own.

Any qualms I had had about our impulsive purchase at the pony auction were now put to rest. Little Fellow was going to be all right.

CHAPTER TEN

Home

ALTHOUGH the four King children and their parents urged us to remain forever with our personable guest, we were anxious to get started on the long trip to Vermont. So, after we'd provided a one-horse show practically beyond the limits of decency, we packed our passenger back in the station wagon. Now we were heading north on the last lap of our journey.

It turned out to be more than a mere trip homeward, though. Little Fellow saw to that.

At one point, for instance, we came to a toll bridge. The rate board indicated that the fee for an automobile and passengers was a dollar. There was also a sign beside the rate board that announced prices from a bygone era:

HORSE AND CONVEYANCE 10¢. EACH PASSENGER 1¢. DRIVER FREE.

The kids nudged me as we drove up to the tollbooth. "Go ahead, Daddy," they said. "I bet you don't dare do it."

Roger gave me a poke as the attendant reached out for the fee. I, in turn, jerked my thumb toward the old sign. "Does that mean what it says?"

It sure did—but where was my horse?

Little Fellow, seeing someone standing next to the car, let out one of his neighs. It was timed perfectly.

The attendant was flabbergasted. His mouth opened, then closed, then opened again. Finally he counted noses, human and otherwise.

And we crossed the bridge for thirteen cents.

Then there was that campground on the Skyline Drive. We arrived after dark. Without really scouting the area thoroughly, we picked a flat spot and unrolled our sleeping bags beneath the stars. Then we tied Little Fellow to a tree at the edge of the clearing.

Our spot, however, proved to be right on a short cut to the rest rooms. Noisy, laughing campers came striding right through the place we'd chosen as our bedroom.

This would never do. But Roger and Little Fellow solved it nicely. Untying his pony, my son relocated him right in the middle of the path. There he remained the rest of the night—a large mysterious Creature, effectively preventing any further use of the short cut. I trust the campers found their way all right by another route.

At sunrise we quickly removed ourselves and our little night watchman from the campground. We figured that dogs and cats were probably frowned on by the National Park Service. If this was the case, ponies might be even more unwelcome. Besides, we wanted to escape anyone who was waiting for daylight to search the pathway for signs of wild beasts.

Now we were really on the final leg of our trip. Late in the afternoon the children began to hail familiar landmarks.

"There's that old barn—still standing!" "Look how tall the corn has grown!" They exclaimed over the sights at each bend in the road, as if we'd been gone for months instead of about two weeks.

Then we rounded the sweeping curve that leads into our little town of Lincoln. We had agreed not to stop at all, but to go right on through to our home two miles the other side of town. So we waved and smiled at our friends in front of the store and on the little lawns as we went by in the fading light.

Finally we rumbled across our bridge. Almost before the car stopped, Roger began lowering the ramp to back his pony out into his new home. As he and Alison walked Little Fellow around the lawn, Peg and I went into the house.

I went to the telephone to let the Douglases know that we had returned, and would pick up our dog, Jack, in the morning. I lifted the receiver—and realized again the joys of Lincoln with its party-line telephones and its small-town neighborliness.

The telephone was already in use by one of the nine other parties who share it with us. ". . . a little horse with them right in the *car*," said a voice.

Yes, we'd made it home. And now that the town knew of the new resident, next day we would have to introduce him to the other members of his new family.

Our patient old shepherd dog was accustomed to all manner of strange creatures in our household. At one time or another he'd had to endure half a dozen raccoons, two skunks, a sparrow hawk with a broken leg, and a misguided muskrat which insisted our house foundation made a better home than the river. When we inherited an orphaned porcupine for a year, Jack had to learn to endure him, too. He patiently accepted the attentions of the little cactus-critter as it crawled up on his back two or three times daily and clung there for a ride.

Since porcupines cannot shoot their quills, and in fact release them only when angry, Jack never once got the equivalent of a burr under his saddle as he served as a mount for his odd little jockey. When Pokey got to weighing ten pounds, however, Jack somehow made him understand that free rides were out.

We felt that such experiences had conditioned Jack for the one he was about to face. Still, we entertained some doubt as to the outcome of their first meeting. After all, from Jack's standpoint Little Fellow was another male animal, even if only a baby. He was about Jack's size, too, so he posed a potential physical threat. But perhaps most important, the pony was receiving a lot of care and attention: Jack might feel that the foal was usurping his place in the family.

Bob and Betty Douglas had had these thoughts, too, so when I told them we would come down to pick up our overgrown lummox, they had other ideas.

"Nothing doing," they said over the telephone. "We want to see the two of them meet. Besides, we want to get a look at your little pony for ourselves."

Thus the next morning the whole Douglas family drove into the yard. Jack was beside himself with joy. He nearly burst out through the window before they got the car door open; he jumped and whined and almost knocked us over. Then, dog fashion, he made the rounds of the yard, visiting his favorite spots and sniffing them carefully to see if, perchance, we had been entertaining strangers.

Gradually his attitude changed. As he investigated the yard his lamblike frolic changed to a halfhearted lope. This, in turn, became a dignified walk. We had hidden Little Fellow in the barn, but Jack's nose told him something was definitely amiss.

Every so often he'd glance at us reproachfully. Although his tongue was still hanging out, it had lost its joyful slobber. We could almost see the smile die on his face.

Finally Jack zeroed in on the barn. His investigation led him to the crack in the barn door with such certainty that he stubbed his nose. And there he stood, sniffing, with only the tip of his tail wagging—uncertain as to what lay beyond the threshold.

"Okay, Jack," Roger grinned, "you found him. Now to let you get acquainted."

We slipped a rope through our pet's collar. Then we retired with him a short distance while Roger led the pony out of the barn.

Seldom have I seen such a change in an animal. Jack, feeling the restraining rope at his neck, stood his ground. Then, slowly, he lay down next to my feet. Ears pricked up, tail stilled now, he watched. Deep in his chest stirred a low growl.

However, the change was not only in Jack. It was in the pony, too. Little Fellow's nose had also told him that there were visitors. He came cautiously out of the barn, searching quickly in all directions. Almost instantly he spied our black-and-white dog.

Without a sound, he whirled. Quick as thought, he dashed behind Roger. There he stood, trembling. His little black-rimmed ears with their white inner fur were pricked forward. His nostrils flared and his eyes were open wide. The hair on his back stood up in a ridge; until then I had never seen hair rise on a horse's back. Plainly this was a wild horse facing the eons-old archenemy of horses—the alert, enormously threatening form of a wolf.

At this moment we realized what a helpless youngster our pony really was. And we realized something else, something that made *my* spine prickly, too. Here, in the fraction of a second, we could visualize the entire history of man's relationship with his two closest friends.

Jack, lying with his furry body actually touching my ankles, had taken his stand with his master. Little Fellow could have been a cave bear or a mastodon. Jack's place was by my side and there he stayed.

The horse has always been, on the other hand, not the hunter but the hunted. Centuries before the first exhausted pony struggled ashore at Assateague, his ancestors had watched for lurking enemies. With the coming of man, horses had thundered across the Asian steppes with the hordes of Genghis Khan. In Arabia, in Europe, perhaps even in earliest North America, they had looked to man for food, support, protection. And so Little Fellow turned to Roger now in his hour of desperate need.

We all stood frozen in pantomime. Then, slowly, the scene relaxed and dissolved. Much, much later I wished I had had my camera to record that fleeting instant. Certainly, even without any prehistoric overtones, it would have made an intriguing picture.

Speaking softly, we gradually introduced the pony to the dog. Leading them both around, we let them get closer to each other. Finally we allowed them to meet. They sniffed noses for a moment, and history was brought up to date. Now that Jack realized the pony was just another of our boarders, he accepted him. The pony, sensing the change in Jack's attitude, did the same. Man's closest friends became friends, too.

After this dramatic confrontation, it was an anticlimax to introduce our pony to the two mares in the pasture. Beauty and ChiChi had heard him whinny a number of times by now, and had answered him. They understood colts, having had a few of their own in the spring of their years. So a few sniffs at each other was all it took.

Within five minutes all three of them were grazing together. Chestnut-colored Beauty, brown-and-white pinto ChiChi and mouse-brown Little Fellow accepted the whole idea. They lived together from then on.

The pony had many other acquaintances to make. Our meadows and woods and river have their share of wild creatures. In fact, they may have more than their share, as we've planted fruit-bearing shrubs for wildlife food, and have allowed our fencerows to grow ragged. These rows shelter such a population of woodchucks, raccoons and skunks as to make my neat-farming Vermont neighbors think my seeming laxity is positively scandalous.

Rabbits often frolic in the greenery of our meadow. Shadowy mink bound furtively along the river. Beavers ferry their poplar branches across the silent pool where they have a bankside home. We've had an ermine on our front porch, coming to a feast of chicken and meat scraps when its tiny stomach was pinched with hunger, the snow lay deep, and the thermometer read twenty below zero.

Therefore it wasn't long before our new family member met some of his wild neighbors. Nearly every one of our animals has encountered a skunk at some time, and Little Fellow was no exception. We didn't happen to witness the meeting, but, as Tom so aptly put it, we got wind of the whole affair.

Almost once a week, from about the middle of February to sometime in November, the air is charged with the musky odor of the harmless little black-and-white pacifists. So we paid no attention when, about six weeks after we'd brought our little pony home, the familiar smell hit our nostrils. However, the next day when we petted our pony, we had all rubbed our hands well into his fur before we really discovered where the odor was coming from.

Probably Little Fellow, in his curiosity, had followed the skunk around as it puttered through the pasture digging for grubs and beetles. Finally, most likely, the pony's attentions had become embarrassing to the wood-pussy, which had been forced to teach Little Fellow what skunks are all about.

By the time we discovered it, the pony was accustomed to the new aura which surrounded him. He was in the doghouse with us for about a week, though, until the bright September sun had deodorized him pretty well. But for weeks after every rain he had that certain aroma.

He met a number of the other animals around the place, too. I know of at least one turtle he followed across a corner of the pasture—although he kept a respectful distance in case it, too, had a surprise for him. And once we saw the three horses standing in a curious circle around an indignant old toad which had somehow been uprooted from its hiding place under a clod of earth.

The most delightful encounter, at least from our viewpoint, came one October morning. The frost lay on the grass and the remaining leaves fell at the first touch of the sun. As usual on arising, we looked out our north window at the horses and their pasture. Beauty and ChiChi were gazing intently up at the edge of the woods. Little Fellow was nowhere to be seen.

Since, after the first few weeks, our pony frequently grazed at some distance from the two mares, we thought nothing of his absence. However, we were curious about what they might be seeing in the woods. We have high respect for the keen visual powers of a horse. No matter how cautiously we emerge from a walk in the woods, for instance, the horses are always looking at us as we discover them. So we figured the horses might be seeing a hiker or hunter.

Then we saw what the horses were watching. Two deer came bounding out of the woods. Leaping high and scarcely seeming to touch the earth between bounds, the first one soon outdistanced its playmate and left it far behind. Then in the early morning mists, it waited for its companion to catch up to it.

Now the chase reversed itself. The pursuer became the pursued, and the game of tag moved once again to the woods.

There was something familiar about that second deer. Snatching my binoculars, I focused on the scene. The first deer was a graceful white-tailed buck, with two little spikes for antlers. The juvenile dots on his coat were still faintly visible when he turned in the sun; he probably was a young-of-the-year who had left his mother's side to make his own way in the world.

The second deer was our own little pony. He tried his best to keep up with his swifter playmate. As I watched the two of them, I realized how perfectly they were matched. Both weighed about a hundred pounds, I judged, and seemed to stand about thirty-six inches high. In fact, as I looked at the unusual scene, I realized that both might well have been born the previous May or June, perhaps even on the same day.

After a while the game was finished. The deer faded into the woodland. Little Fellow came out into the pasture and began grazing as if nothing unusual had happened.

This is the only time any of our horses have actively associated with deer, that I know of. But we may see the slender wild creatures in the same pasture with them at any time of the year.

Although I never expect to watch a horse and a deer play together again, such contacts are by no means rare in our Green Mountains, where man lives but a step from the woods. A neighbor of mine in Lincoln has known a ruffed grouse to enter his chickenyard and start fights with the rooster. Many a Vermont farm pond bears odd-looking ducks that are obviously the result of a family reunion between a wild mallard and a domestic quacker. And a farmer in Monkton noted a pair of antlers sticking out of the center of his herd of cattle one morning as they came to the barn. When the cows entered a lane that would admit only one or two animals at a time, the antlers—complete with magnificent white-tailed buck attached—sailed easily over the fence and disappeared across the fields.

It wasn't long after his romp with the deer that Little Fellow made the acquaintance of others of his own kind. The occasion was the Annual Fall Horse Show and Gymkhana in East Middlebury, Vermont.

Already our pony was too large to go to the show in his traveling stall. So, with Roger riding in the back to steady him, he just stood in the middle of the microbus without it.

Frankly, you can have your horse shows. As if all that creaking leather, blaring noise and dust aren't bad enough, they charge you to park your car. And then they charge you to get inside the gate. However, since Little Fellow was going to be in it, I went along. But I felt like a father at a kindergarten graduation.

Little Fellow shared none of my reluctance. Long before the bus bumped to a stop on the grassy parking lot, he'd smelled the presence of the other horses. He gave a long whinny that Roger said "almost took my ears off, Dad." Then, after we'd led him out of the VW, he spent the next few minutes on the alert.

He became the immediate center of attention. Arching his neck, he pranced like a little circus pony. And I must confess that I enjoyed basking in his reflected glory. Even though the dust and the leather and loudspeakers were still there, it was different when your own flesh and blood was on display.

Of course, being only about four months of age, he'd had no training. The only class he could enter was the one listed in the program as for Yearlings or Less.

We watched Roger lead him to the center of the ring with the others. Little Fellow was the smallest, being just under forty inches—or, to use the proper parlance, ten hands—in height at the withers. The announcer told Little Fellow's story briefly, pronouncing "Chincoteague" the way we'd heard it most of the time while we were on the island, with the *ch* hard as in "church."

A woman took her place beside me at the rail. "Which one is supposed to be the Chincoteague pony?" she asked.

I pointed to Roger and Little Fellow.

The woman shook her head. "Maybe," she said. "But I doubt it. Chincoteague ponies are all spotted and pinto-colored. This one's a mousey brown."

"Fawn," I suggested.

"And besides," she continued, silencing me with a look, "they don't even know how to pronounce the name. It's supposed to be '*Shin*coteague.' "

I was about to say more, but Peg jabbed me in the ribs. Then the woman produced the clincher. "Furthermore," she declared, "that little impostor doesn't look as if he's even weaned yet. How'd they ever get something like that clear up here from Virginia?"

How indeed? Before I could answer, the woman steered herself away to spread the tidings of our fraud elsewhere through the crowd.

But our "little impostor" cleared himself. Although we had to admit that he was no show pony, he managed to pick up fourth prize. Which, as Roger said as he hung up the white ribbon later, was pretty good for a colt that had had to walk, swim and ride more than a thousand miles to get to the horse show.

It was after we had retired our prize-winner for the season that a sneaky little question which had been bothering us came to the fore. Now that he'd taken all the laurels he probably would garner until he was big enough to ride, just what was going to be his position around our hundred acres?

From the looks of his relatives down there in Virginia, he never would be much of a show pony. He had plenty of good plain sturdiness; but he would need more than this to win in competition against carefully bred individuals having fine heads and classic conformation. We had no doubt that he was smart and willing enough to learn to perform well in equestrian classes—perhaps even in dressage, or to do tricks. But this meant training and practice and long hours of riding. And, while Roger was the right size and temperament for him now, it would take another two or three years before Little Fellow was right for Roger to ride. And by then our son would be in his early teens, when he was likely to have outgrown his pony.

However, we knew one thing: Little Fellow was not going to become a mere curiosity. Somewhere along the line his place in our scheme of things would be worked out.

Meanwhile Roger proceeded to carry out his part of the bargain made at the auction. Alison volunteered to help raise some of the money, so they figured out various ways to earn fifty dollars. Roger raked leaves around the town, lined up a few jobs shoveling snow, and sold magazine subscriptions. Alison set aside a portion of her babysitting money, made fudge and sold it, and earned a little money picking apples.

One Saturday, as we were preparing a stall for Little Fellow in the barn, some of Roger's friends came to see if he wanted to play football. He sighed and said he guessed he'd better keep working on the stall with me.

After they were gone he sighed again. "Gosh, Dad, it's easy to buy things, but it's hard to pay for them, isn't it?"

I glanced at the Volkswagen out in the driveway, and considered the washing machine and electric stove in the house. Thank heaven these, at last, were ours. Yet I winced inwardly as Roger's remark brought back memories.

Then, as we got back to work, it occurred to me that perhaps here was something our pony could do better than any of the other animals around the farm: He could give my children some basic information about the "buy now, pay later" way of doing things.

And if only they remembered it longer than their parents had managed to do, that pony would turn out to be one of the best horse-trades they ever could make.

CHAPTER ELEVEN

Mistaken Identity

"DADDY, what's the matter with Little Fellow?" I glanced up from my newspaper to see Alison's troubled face.

"He's just standing there. And he's got a great big lump on his neck."

Alison has always been the most compassionate one of the family. Once, when she was small, she brought in a wounded warbler she'd found by the side of the road. It died while she cradled it in her hands. Later I discovered her making a soft

111

little casket for it, tears streaming down her cheeks. Then she buried it out on our front lawn. The little mound can still be seen there today. And every autumn is a time of new heartbreak as she listens for the forlorn song of the last grasshopper in the meadow.

So I wasn't as concerned as I might have been by her question about the pony. Probably he had been bitten by a fly, I told her, and it had swollen like a mosquito bite.

"But a lump as big as a baseball?"

I shaped the size with my hands. "*That* big?"

"Oh, yes. And it's got a cut, and everything. Come see."

I thought of what could possibly have happened as I followed her out to the pasture. One of the hazards faced by almost every domestic animal in Vermont is that of running afoul of a porcupine. These waddling rodents, the size of a cocker spaniel, are common in New England. Normally they are confined to the trees where they chew twigs and bark, but they are independent enough to wander across an open pasture at any time. Approached by another animal, a porcupine defends itself by hunching up, head tucked down for protection, and presenting a bristle of sharp spines from nose to tail.

The appearance of a porcupine on the defensive seems to intrigue other animals; they apparently can't resist nosing such an unusual bundle. And, although unable to "throw" its quills, it can lash out with a prickly tail and leave several dozen stilettos imbedded in its surprised visitors. I have seen dogs, cats, even cows with so many gray-black quills in their muzzles that they look as if they had frosty mustaches. It's a job to pull the quills, too: they are barbed, working steadily deeper with every movement, and the operation of removing them can be extremely painful to the victim.

I doubted that our pony's trouble had anything to do with porcupines, however. If such had been the case, he would be more likely to be injured on his nose than on his neck. Perhaps the experience of a friend came closer to what might have happened.

He kept some ponies on a farm a few miles away. One day he noted that his little stallion had a long gash on its rump. Looking closer, he discovered that there were four other gashes paralleling the first; they sliced right down the thickest part of the rump for nearly fourteen inches. A black bear had made a lunge for the pony, and had succeeded in a near miss.

We knew there were bears in the woods around us. Often when walking through the forest I would see a beech tree whose smooth bark showed clearly the presence of the animals. There would be an ascending series of deep-dug claw marks as the creature shinnied up for the tender beechnuts. The blackberry patch at the upper end of our farm would be matted and stripped of its fruit every fall by bears, too. And every now and then we had come across an anthill pulled apart, or a rotten log shredded all over the landscape for its grubs.

It was not impossible that our pony had been attacked by a bear. It didn't seem likely so near the house, but when we approached Little Fellow I could see that something very wrong indeed had happened to him.

Alison hadn't exaggerated. He had a gouge in his skin. And the swelling on his neck was even bigger than a baseball. It was more like a grapefruit. This was no mosquito bite.

Gently I touched the area around the wound. Little Fellow made no move. "See?" Alison said. "He hardly notices us. He just stands there."

There was something in her words that set me thinking. And as I stood and considered further, a chill went down my spine.

"Alison," I said softly, putting my arm around her shoulders, "come away."

As we walked toward the house, I tried to make light of it. No use alarming her until I'd talked with a veterinarian. So I told her it was probably where he'd been scratched by a thorn.

I sent her on some little errand while I called the veterinarian. "Doc," I said, "what's it like when a horse has rabies?"

The papers had carried several stories about the possibility of rabies among wild animals in the summer. So far I hadn't heard of any cases reported in our section of Vermont, but there could always be a first time. And what little I knew of the disease indicated that any animal which appeared listless or stupefied should be left strictly alone.

Even though it is commonly considered to be a disease of dogs, rabies can strike any warm-blooded animal, from chipmunks to cows. It is generally passed from one to another through a bite. Little Fellow, with his inborn curiosity, might have walked up to a rabid raccoon and been infected with that dreadful saliva before he could save himself.

I told the veterinarian of my fears. Yet even as we talked they began to melt away. After all, he assured me, rabies may take weeks to develop in an animal after exposure. Although at the moment I couldn't recall when we'd last seen our pony in perfect health, the gash looked fairly fresh. Three or four days old, at the most. So, even if we had a wounded horse on our hands, at least we didn't have a mad pony.

If it wasn't hydrophobia, though, what was it he did have? The doctor had been on his way to an emergency call when I 'phoned, and wouldn't be able to get to us for a couple of hours. But he took the time to help me consider the possibilities.

"Couldn't be one of those trigger-happy hunters up in your area, could it?" he asked. "Some of those guys'll shoot anything that moves. An animal that was creased by a bullet could be dazed. It might just snap out of it, and everything will be okay."

Maybe, I agreed. But how come the lump? And anyway, how come they'd shoot a pony?

He reminded me that I would have a lump, too, if I was

whacked just right by a bullet. "And as for why they'd shoot a pony, Ron, I've had farmers call me and say somebody had shot their best heifer. Some idiot probably took it for a deer. Which reminds me—what color is that pony of yours?"

I winced as I told him. "Mouse—I mean fawn—brown."

"See? There you are. But I'm just guessing until I get a look at your pony. I'll be there as soon as I can."

Not long after I had hung up, Alison burst into the room. "He's walking! Daddy, he's better! Please—let's go see!"

Little Fellow was ambling along in the pasture as if nothing was wrong. That crease just could have been made by a bullet. This was what the vet decided, too, after he arrived and examined him.

With nearly seventy percent of Vermont in woodland, there is scarcely a spot that isn't covered eventually by some hunter looking for woodchucks, rabbits, raccoons or other game. Being the fall, there were now more hunters than ever. And in less than two months there would be still more. Then thousands of hunters from all over the northeastern United States and Canada would roam the Vermont forests for a glimpse of the tawny coat of a white-tailed deer.

At the same time and right there in the pasture would be about a hundred pounds of deer-colored Chincoteague pony—slender of body and swift of foot. But we knew he'd never be swift enough to escape the bullet of the hunter who forgot to look for antlers before he squeezed the trigger.

I had bought the pony as a gesture of love for Roger. For our own satisfaction we had brought him away from his home in the wildlife refuge. And now this.

What had happened was as surely my responsibility as if I had fired that shot myself. And that pony, bought so impulsively, would remain my responsibility for years to come.

Even if his present wound had been only an accident, there

was but one thing to do. Creature of the outdoors though he was, he would have to be put in the barn. At least during deer season.

"He's beautiful," lamented Roger, "but why does he have to be that color?"

Of course there was no answer—except to put the finishing touches to his little stall in the barn.

CHAPTER TWELVE

New Friends

W<small>HILE</small> we worried about Little Fellow's safety, he quietly proceeded to do something about it himself. He developed acne.

Naturally, it wasn't the same blotchy skin that makes the lives of teenagers miserable, but it looked a lot like it. His coat of mouse brown began to fall out.

Janice first noticed it one mid-October weekend when she came home from college. "What on earth's happening to our pony?" she asked. "Did you dye his hair and forget to rinse him?"

We took a look. She was right: he was positively weird.

117

It is normal for most animals to put on heavier fur at the end of summer. But with a few exceptions, such as the snowshoe hare and the weasel, which swap a brown summer coat for winter's white, most of the animals we know keep the same color scheme.

Not so with Little Fellow, however. He looked as if somebody had been throwing mud at him. That fawn-colored coat was splotched and ragged, and where the hair had fallen out a new darker crop was showing. He was becoming two-toned. For days he walked around in his checkered garment. We almost felt like turning away so he wouldn't catch us looking at him.

Then, as the darker fur became predominant, we saw that our pony's complexion was clearing. Not only was he losing his summer coat, he was also losing his baby fur. The new coat which appeared was long and lustrous, and so remarkably dense that we could hardly part the hairs enough to see his light-colored skin.

In making this change, of course, he was merely being a Chincoteague pony. Even in the southerly latitude of Virginia, the wintry days would be mighty chilly on the sea-swept beach. Several hundred years of wild ancestry were providing our pony with the protection he would need. And his heavy coat would come in handy for our Vermont winter, too.

We breathed more easily as our colt turned from a mouse-brown to a luxuriant dark chocolate. Now, at least, he was the wrong color for a deer. We wouldn't have to shut him in the barn after all.

As this point the pony showed another sign of his Chincoteague ancestry. As the pasture had become poorer, we had let down one fence after another to allow our horses wider room to forage for food. Finally we let them wander anywhere they wished, because those five hundred bales of hay we had stored in the barn represented a cost of about fifty cents a bale, and we weren't anxious to start winter feeding any earlier than necessary.

Little Fellow took cheerfully to the restricted diet. He left the fading grass to the mares and began to nibble twigs, exactly as his relatives were probably doing back in Virginia.

One day around the first of November I went out to prune my blueberry bushes, only to find that our pony had already pruned them. Alarmed, I went over to a few apple trees I'd set out a couple of years previously. Sure enough, he'd been there before me. He'd also pruned the little weeping willow tree which Peg had raised from a cutting. The small pear trees and the silver maples had that crew-cut appearance, too.

At this turn of events I recalled the comforting remark of a fireman at the auction. "Oh, they're easy-keepers. Your pony'll learn to eat almost anything."

At least here was one hoss-trade where the goods had not been misrepresented. Not one bit. I walked out to where our little Virginian was helping himself to some Vermont raspberry twigs. "Okay, you 'easy-keeper,' you," I said ruefully as I snapped a rope to his halter. "Nothing but baled hay and store-bought grain for you from now on."

Thus decked out in fur coat and appetite, Little Fellow began his first winter. Like Beauty and ChiChi, who had developed fairly heavy coats of their own, he actually preferred to be outdoors. We left the stable door open, but they'd enter only in bitter weather.

This system of letting the horses decide what they liked got us in bad with a pair of dear ladies. They drove sedately across our bridge one wintry day.

"We came to see your pony," they announced. Not knowing who they were, but having had a number of other strangers arrive with the same request, I took them out to the pasture.

The horses were all standing in the February sunshine, eating the hay I had placed in the outdoor feeding racks. "Do they always stay out here?" one of the women asked.

I told them that all three spent the greater part of their time in the vicinity of the racks. "In fact," I added, trying to be helpful, "they've not been in the barn for about two weeks now."

"Not even the pony?"

I shook my head. "Not even the pony."

At this, both visitors looked grim. After a few more questions they asked to see the barn. So I showed them the stall, with its door fastened open and hay still in the mangers. Obviously the horses could go in if they wished.

They thanked me and drove away as sedately as they had come. I thought nothing more of their visit. But about two weeks later in Middlebury I stopped to chat with a State Police trooper whom I know. "By the way," he said, "in case you were wondering— we investigated that complaint about your horses."

"What complaint?"

"That you weren't taking care of them. I went out there last week, but you all were away. So I took the liberty of looking around a bit. And for a starving horse, you've got the fattest little pony I ever saw."

Not all of our visitors, of course, are quite like those who reported my cruelty to animals. Far more often they are a carload of wonderful people who have heard about our star boarder through a friend.

"We came to see your Chincoteague pony," the driver will announce hopefully as four or five eager young faces peer beyond me toward the pasture. After introductions have been passed around, one of us takes them on the little tour. Eventually we'll discover Beauty and ChiChi—and Little Fellow.

The reaction is always the same. Predictably, wonderfully, the same. "Oh!" they'll exclaim, "isn't he beautiful!" It doesn't matter if he's just a dot in the far end of the pasture; to their eyes our pony is beautiful no matter how far away he may be.

At my call, Little Fellow comes trotting up to the fence. We pat him and talk to him and give him a piece of apple or carrot.

And always they want to hear his story. Finally, after more petting and "he's beautifuls," they reluctantly take their leave.

Although such visits often interrupt whatever we were doing, we have never begrudged the time. Not one bit. The shine in the eyes of the youngsters—and often in the eyes of their parents—brightens up all the rest of our day.

Photographers have come to take movies of Little Fellow. Artists have come to paint him. One man who went up into our north pasture to do a landscape put the three horses in his picture. Beauty and ChiChi remained chestnut and pinto, respectively, but Little Fellow underwent a sea-change. He emerged as a palomino stallion with golden coat and flowing white mane.

Some of our visitors have become real friends. Gilbert and Kathleen Sladen, who saw Little Fellow in a slide show I gave at a lodge in Stowe, came to see him for themselves; last spring we returned the visit at their home in Creemore, Ontario. And the gracious owner of the lodge at which the slides were shown was none other than Maria von Trapp, of *Sound of Music* fame. She had read about our pony and asked to see the pictures. So now I number her as a friend, too.

If we decide to go to Alaska, British Columbia or Mexico, we have more friends waiting for us there. We've never met them, but we feel as if we know them just the same. Little Fellow has introduced us through the medium of some pictures they've seen in one of my talks, perhaps, or something I've written. Our acquaintance has ripened through correspondence.

In exchanging letters we have learned about some of the other ponies like Little Fellow. A woman near Boston has rigged out a little cart for her grandchildren so her little Chincoteaguer can take the youngsters for a ride when they come to visit. A man in Indiana has several of them; he's trained one to do a number of tricks, such as to nod for "yes" or "no," pick out which hat hides the apple—and bow deeply when the spectators applaud.

Most of the pony-owners point out that a horse three-quarters the size of usual riding horses needs only three-quarters of their space to keep him. Actually he needs even less, if you consider the weeds and twigs and miscellaneous greenery he'll eat if he gets the chance.

And one owner in Pennsylvania wrote to me: "Trixie is the best souvenir we've ever brought home from a trip. She may have cost more than a salamander at a circus, but what can you do with a salamander?"

Among Little Fellow's visitors was an individual who arrived more than a year ago. And, as I write this, he still is here. He's a racing Thoroughbred, retired from the track by some people near Boston who had heard of our little pony, and wondered if we thought we could make room for a big, good-natured "also-ran."

The idea was an instant success: Little Fellow took to Yankee at once. In a way, he had no choice, for the lanky runner was twice his size. But since that date the two have been fast friends.

The big Thoroughbred couldn't have come at a better time. Beauty and ChiChi had become too old and dignified for such foolishness as being herded into a two-mare harem by a teen-ager who might be feeling his oats. Now Little Fellow can work off some of his boisterousness by nipping and snorting at Yankee. The larger horse patiently endures his small friend's playfulness, or nips him back if he gets too rough.

Yet even though he spends most of his time communing with Yankee, he remains one of the family. He still comes running when one of us appears at the pasture fence. Then we scratch his ears and sometimes give him a piece of carrot.

At three years of age and about thirteen hands (fifty-two inches) in height, Little Fellow has probably attained his full growth. Occasionally Roger or Alison climbs on his back and rides him around the yard. We figure that at last he is big enough so real people—albeit rather small ones—can be substituted for the sand-filled bags which formerly we had placed on his back to get him used to the notion of carrying the weight of a rider.

However, one question still arises, even though it is more in the minds of our visitors than in our own thoughts: Exactly what can you *do* with him?

"What can you do with a dog or a cat?" I could counter. "What can you do with a baby? Of what value is a lawn?"

Actually the question would scarcely be entertained at all if they lived with Little Fellow as we have. He is definitely an individual in his own right, not merely a rare kind of pony.

He has given up at least one of his Chincoteague ways, and shows a decided preference for grass over twigs. This makes us breathe easier for our shrubbery when we let him roam loose in the fall.

On the other hand, his familiarity with water has allowed him to do something that even Yankee does not attempt. When I go out of the house on a fall morning to mail some letters, Little Fellow follows me right across the bridge to the mailbox. Then he turns and follows me back. The same trip with a balking and jittery Yankee would take about five minutes, each way. Horses just don't like bridges.

Little Fellow amuses us with his curiosity, too. As a rule we don't allow him to run around the yard in summer, but one day he got out of the pasture. None of us knew of his escape until Peg was suddenly aware that she had company while she was reading the newspaper in her lawn chair. Little Fellow had quietly walked up and was contemplating her from about four feet away.

Because his hoofs are harder than those of the mares and the Thoroughbred, he needs no shoes and hence has escaped the professional notice of the local blacksmith. But this didn't keep him out of the proceedings one time when Mr. LeBoeuf paid us his visit. Whereas we had to capture the other horses and lead them to the stall, the pony obligingly went into the barn and stood waiting near by. When Mr. LeBoeuf bent to his work, though, we had to make sure all doors were closed—to keep the other horses in, and to keep Little Fellow out.

Then, too, we have realized his importance to us ever since the time he was taken sick because he ate too many wild apples. I decided that wild apple trees weren't very common on Chincoteague, so he didn't have any inbred caution signals about them. His sickness, despite being probably little more than an upset stomach, affected us all.

At this writing, three years after we brought him home to meet the old-timers at the farm, Little Fellow has at last come into his own.

One of the heartbreaking things about having animals is that some day you must part with them. We have lost our old dog, Jack. ChiChi has gone to the home of Charlie and Jackie Phillips, where she can live out her few remaining months near the place of her birth. Beauty's old teeth got to bothering her so much that it became an ordeal for her to eat; reluctantly, we have had her put to sleep. Thus in three short years Little Fellow has become our senior-animal-in-residence, although Yankee is chronologically older than he is.

Now it is our Chincoteague pony who passes judgment on the procession of creatures that continues to pass through our place. He allowed Hezekiah, one of the seven raccoons we've had, to wander around his feet last winter whenever he was in the barn and Hezzy would wake up from his fitful hibernation among the hay bales. He quivered, but stood his ground, when Sparky, our gray squirrel, leapt from my shoulder to his back. And he has sniffed curiously at Volans, the flying squirrel which was given to me after being injured in a neighbor's barn by a cat.

Most of these animals have come to me from local sources. However, I have told my friends at several zoos and city parks to give me first refusal if they happen to have an extra animal on hand.

Therefore it was no surprise when Dr. Herbert Knoblach, at the Bronx Zoo, telephoned me recently to ask if I was coming down to New York sometime soon.

"Why, yes, as a matter of fact. End of next week."

"Great. We've got a gentle, denatured little skunk. She's a wonderful creature, but she can never be let loose because she has no defense in the wild. Want her, Ron?"

And so I must be off for New York City. As I go to pick up Rosebud and bring her back, in my mind's eye I can see Little Fellow waiting for me. When the bridge rumbles its greeting, those white-lined ears will prick up. Then he'll come forward to inspect the latest, newest member of the family, and extend to her that which he received three years ago: a welcome to our hundred acres.

ABOUT THE AUTHOR

As a small boy in Connecticut, Ronald Rood learned from his parents to love and respect wild creatures, and he was only seven years old when a personal letter from his idol, Thornton Burgess, inspired him to become a naturalist himself. He received his Bachelor of Science degree from the University of Connecticut in 1941, and worked a gold claim in Alaska until Pearl Harbor, whereupon he joined the Air Force and became a fighter pilot over Europe. After the war he returned to the University for his M.S. in wildlife management, and married his laboratory assistant, the former Peg Bruce. In 1953 the Roods and their four children moved to their hundred acres in Lincoln, Vermont, which have become a nature preserve familiar to readers throughout North America.

Now a full-time author and lecturer, he has written six natural history books for children, articles for *Reader's Digest, Audubon Magazine,* and *Christian Herald,* and is a regular contributor to *Vermont Life.* His two earlier adult titles, LAND ALIVE and THE LOON IN MY BATHTUB, were chosen as a dual selection by the Natural Science Book Club in 1966.

INDEX

INDEX